Introducing:

Visual Identities for
Small Businesses

gestalten

Introducing.

Visual Identities for Small Businesses

Business people are run by the left-hand side of their brain, designers by the right-hand side. So they say. In the golden — or rather multi-colored — age of entrepreneurship, setting up a business appears to be a creative task in its own right. Inventive, unexpected business models are key, as is flexibility.

Anna Day and Ellie Jauncy worked in the fields of fashion design and illustration before they founded a full-service flower shop. ✦ p. 250 Jon Contino and Matt Gorton quit their design studio to establish their own clothing line. ✦ p. 163 Daniel Martinavarro teamed up with his sister, the designer Rocío Martinavarro, to develop a meaningful identity for his bakery shop. ✦ p. 184 And the designers of the Studio Goodmorning Technology develop and sell bicycle parts under the label of a side project that they branded theirselves. ✦ p. 106

Professions are certainly not to be set in stone and although each job description still demands a very different set of competences, areas of overlap are becoming larger and more evident. An increasing number of job-hoppers, side jobs, redeployment and extra-occupational re-training schemes are blurring the borders between the various business sectors and areas of expertise. Skill bases turn into variables that are not only continuously advanced and enhanced, but also readjusted and redefined.

At some point, all those who run a company find themselves confronted with the tricky task of translating the essence of their business model into a coherent corporate image. *Introducing* focuses in on entrepreneurs who assail this task with growing confidence; on creative, hands-on business people who understand the benefits of good design, enjoy the process of making, and are prepared to invest a surprising amount of time and effort on their company's public presentation.

As the impact of visual communications increases, the responsibility of corporate design reaches beyond traditional printed matter into business management. Responsibilities blur, especially when it comes to small companies and start ups. Generally speaking, corporate design is the product of a collaboration between business and design. The success of the corporate image depends on the strength of this collaboration, on the closeness and integrity of the relationship. The selection in this book seeks to survey such relationships, and it does so with a keen awareness of the fact that the product changes when roles are shifting. When creative tasks are carried out by the business side. When the relationship is personal, rather than business-related. And of course in the rare cases in which there is no professional designer involved at all.

Some of the entrepreneurs featured in this book developed their brand image under their own steam, some collaborated to give shape to their concept, taking the time and effort to pass valuable insights into the culture of their business on to a professional designer. What they certainly did not do is buy a recipe-like theory or across-the-counter solution from a branding agency, assign the job, and turn away. They stayed in touch. Because they understand that branding is personal identification as much as it is public presentation.

And that a visual identity can only be reasonably developed if both sides of the brain act jointly.

Both from a business and a design perspective, start-ups and small businesses constitute a creative playground for experimentation. The beauty of this selection lies in the variety of its themes and styles. The chapter "Sunny Side Up" features experimental approaches from frisky and playful to bold and adventurous. "Pretty Straight" portrays examples of concise and reductionist branding solutions. "Everlasting" surveys the return to traditional values and handcrafted elements as a new direction in contemporary corporate design. Finally, "With a Twist" gathers conceptual solutions that take a lateral, often unexpected approach to the challenge of developing an effective visual identity.

Intelligent branding is certainly not peculiar to any particular trade, so the projects showcased in this book are not structured by business sectors. *Introducing* highlights the personal nature of branding and presents corporate identity as a form of self-conception. Although grounded in commercial realities, the book turns away from general merchandise and industry classifications, portrays an art gallery next to a cardiologist and a dog walker, a hoola hoop performance artist next to an organic farm. It turns towards brand expression, brand experience, and the art of exceptional solutions.

◆ Anna Sinofzik

A   Sunny Side Up

B   Pretty Straight

C   Everlasting

D   With a Twist

Pino, pp. 18–19

Sun‑ny‑ Side Up

Starting a business can certainly be a painstaking endeavor. But it can also be an exciting venture and a whole lot of fun. Branding can be fun, too, both with regard to the creative process and to the brand itself as a product and experience. The most obvious characteristic elements for a "fun branding" are vivid colors, exuberant textures, diverse patterns, and illustrations. But of course, there is not just the playful, friendly kind of fun, but also the harshly ironic, glaringly bold, and daringly experimental. A fresh, intrepid approach is key and the unifying characteristic of this section.

The selection here is a refreshing counterbalance to the current atmosphere of gloom and uncertainty in the business world. It includes projects and brands that may appear unexpected in this context and shows that a vivid visual language is by no means intrinsically tied to particular fields or business sectors. Pirol's branding solution for Munt la Reita, + p. 42 Hyperkit's for Jo&Co, + p. 30 and Raw Color's for Keukenkonfessies + p. 20 exemplify how a playful approach that may appear clichéd, overdone and perfect for a kindergarten, can be surprisingly powerful and no less suitable for an organic farm, a hairdresser, or a food design studio. It is not about being naive or a quirky maverick by hook or by crook, but about being confident.

Confidence—at least the well-founded kind—requires a good understanding of the market and a good deal of self-reflection. Manifiesto Futura's branding for Robertson Printing + p. 44 portrays typical visual elements of the trade in a flashy and unconventional way. The result stands out and makes a lasting impression on potential clients that may otherwise have overlooked the company. Cobbenhagen & Hendriksen developed an authentic, unpretentious brand language for Buitenwerkplaats, + p. 43 a refurbished farm that provides temporary workspaces for professionals of various disciplines. Simple cloud and tree illustrations represent the company's primary feature of the surrounding rural idyll and at the same time imply authenticity and honesty, features that are rare to find in a world of nifty marketing and overblown brand strategies. Mind Design's corporate identity for Marawa the Amazing + p. 40 suggests entertainment and delight, matching the core values of the hoola-hoop artist's offerings.

The trick is to be well-grounded but unexpected, knowledgeable but unmediated and refreshingly forthright, not to mince matters but to shout it out and still be deemed trustworthy. Each brand has a voice, but some are louder than others.

THEUREL & THOMAS

THEUREL & THOMAS

EUREL & THOMAS

THEUREL & THOMAS

Denise Theurel Thomas
NO.350 | L.17
E-MAIL
denise@theurelandthomas.com

t 8356 0113
Avenida Calzada del Valle / Plaza las Villas
San Pedro Garza García, NL, Mx

Theurel & Thomas

San Pedro Garza García, Mexico

<u>Anagrama</u>, 2009

Theurel & Thomas is the very first pâtisserie in Mexico to specialize in French macarons. To emphasize the unique value of the delicate dessert, Anagrama created a brand identity that contrasts the colorful macarons with a mostly white backdrop and classic black type. Cyan and magenta are only interspersed here and there as an abstract reference to the French flag.

"White was our primary designtool. As a result, all the attention is drawn to the colorful macarons."

Frozen Dutch

Amsterdam, Netherlands

Ewoudt Boonstra, 2011

Frozen Dutch is what its name suggests: a Dutch ice cream brand. Like the artistic movement De Stijl, Frozen Dutch stands for elementarism—in this context pure flavors and honest brand communications. The logo is in the shape of an ice cream scoop, its colors are those of different flavors, and the business card is an ice cream stick. The designer Ewoudt Boonstra is the creative force behind Frozen Dutch's corporate image.

WE ARE FROZEN. WE ARE DUTCH. HENCE THE NAME.

BUT THOSE AREN'T THE ONLY TWO WORDS THAT DESCRIBE US. FAR FROM IT. WE COULD HAVE CALLED OURSELVES CREAMY AWESOMENESS. BECAUSE OF THE PURE, NATURAL DAIRY THAT WE GET FROM HAPPY DUTCH COWS. OR BIOLOGICAL FRIEND-O. BECAUSE WE USE ONLY THE FINEST, CERTIFIED BIO-INGREDIENTS, WITHOUT EXCEPTION. OR SEASON'S EATINGS. BECAUSE OUR FLAVORS CHANGE WITH THE SEASONS AND THE FRESH INGREDIENTS EACH BRINGS. OR WHAT ABOUT MOUTHWATERING TASTY, NATURAL MINDBLOWER, YUM YUMMY...?...? WE COULD KEEP GOING. BUT, IN THE END, THE NAME ON THE CARTON DOESN'T REALLY MATTER, DOES IT? IT'S THE COLD STUFF ON THE INSIDE THAT COUNTS. AND WE HAPPEN TO BELIEVE IN OUR COLD STUFF VERY MUCH. THAT'S WHY WE GUARANTEE THE FRESHNESS AND DELICIOUSNESS OF EACH BITE.

Super by Dr. Nicholas Perricone

San Francisco, USA

Concrete, 2010

Dr. Nicholas Perricone is a board certified clinical and research dermatologist. A beauty guru to the stars. He is also the author of the three *New York Times* No. 1 best sellers, *The Perricone Promise, The Perricone Prescription,* and *The Wrinkle Cure.* His most recent success is the decision to rebrand his skincare brand "Perricone MD" into "Super." The new identity concept was developed by Concrete and is based on the nutritional ingredients of "superfoods," a term coined by Dr. Perricone himself to describe foods that contain significant amounts of antioxidants. Apart from being an obvious reference to the superfood science of the product, the name sets the overall tone of the brand: super design, super packaging, super consumer advertising, super website design, super boutiques with point-of-sale graphics. The first Super boutique opened in Berkeley, California in 2010; a global expansion is in the works.

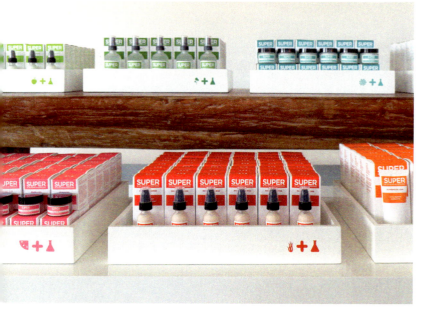

UO
Make—Up

Philadelphia, USA

Pure Magenta, 2010

UO Make-Up is not really a small business, but the debut make-up line of the major fashion conglomerate Urban Outfitters. With the aim of establishing a sub-brand that would have its own voice and the aesthetic of a spunky little start-up, Urban Outfitters approached Pure Magenta, who developed a highly individual range of beauty collateral based on a certain beauty editorial iconography. The logo mark resembles a seal of make-up containing symbols of a deconstructed face.

However independent its style, UO Make-Up is designed to subtly complement Urban Outfitters' products and graphics and form a part of the greater whole.

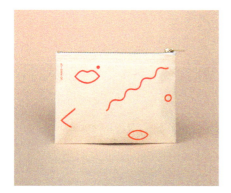

Aschen
and Voss

Geneva, Switzerland

Established NYC, 2010

Aschen and Voss is a Swiss newcomer brand in the beauty and cosmetics industry.

Geared towards the sophisticated, adult consumer, the identity and packaging by Established NYC manages to combine the sterility of pharmaceutics and Swiss purity of form with an attractive, gentle feel.

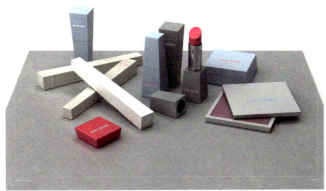

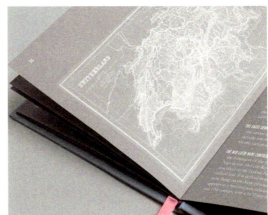

17

Pino

Helsinki, Finland

Bond, 2010

Pino is Finnish for "pile" or "stack." The branding concept for the Helsinki-based interior decoration shop Pino picks up on the meaning of its name: A stack of lines form the letter "i" in the logotype, while stacked shelves and simple storage racks serve as shop fixtures. A range of vivid colors and patterns reflect the diversity of Pino's product range.

"Pino offers a refreshing product range that combines personality, practicality, and design. We believe that our fun and functional approach to everyday products has a positive impact on ourselves and our environment."

Sunny Side Up

Keuken-
confessies

Eindhoven, Netherlands

Raw Color, 2010

Keukenconfessies (Kitchen Confessions) is Maarten Lockefeer's and Franke Elshout's food design studio in Eindhoven. Having met in the small kitchen of a restaurant called De Bommel (Lockefeer was the chef, Elshout the dishwasher trying to pay her way through design school), they decided to start up for themselves. Combining the skills of cooking and design, they develop concepts that get people to enjoy food and to interact with what they're eating.

Raw Color applied Keukenconfessies experimental, open approach to eatables and to their design. The result is a vivid and playful corporate image. Instead

of one definite logo mark, Raw Color created a diverse set of colorful, foody icons. Like ingredients in the kitchen, these can be mixed and combined to form an infinite variety of creations. Plain black typography contrasts the naive aesthetics of the illustrations. One layer of the business cards is stamped on manually—handcrafted, just like Keukenconfessies products.

21

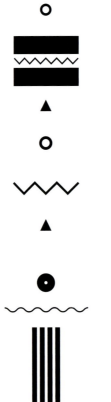

ZPYZ

Berlin, Germany

<u>Hort</u>, 2010

ZPYZ is a Berlin-based music project. Having put their name on the map with hard-to-define remixes for Mando Diao, Polarkreis 18, and Rosenstolz they asked Hort to translate their music into graphics and help them become established as a visual brand. The resulting corporate image is based on unpredictable geometry. A series of basic shapes offers diverse possibilities for alternate arrangements and layouts and spontaneous variation. An old photocopier was used to generate a nice grittiness and a pleasant contrast to the clean geometric forms.

22

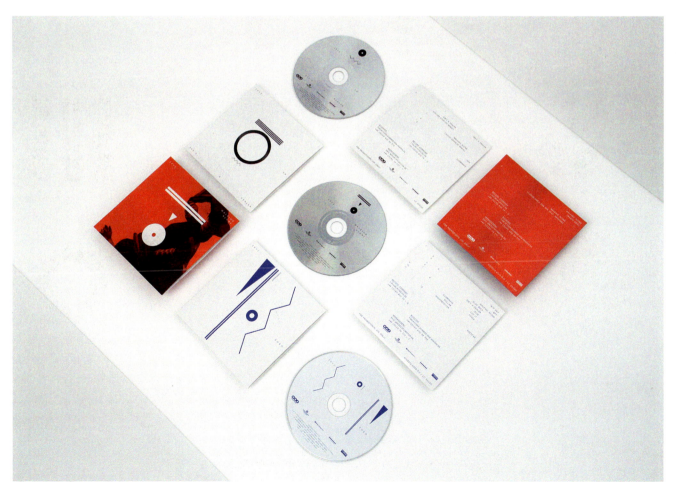

Atelier Punkt

Montreal, Canada

Feed, 2008

The privately run gallery space Atelier Punkt opened its doors in Montreal in 2008. Since then, it has showcased emerging graphic and object design, architecture, photography, and illustration, particularly focusing on creatives from the Quebec region. As a multidisciplinary artist herself, founder Melinda Pap set great value upon the visual representation of her venture and approached Feed with its realization.

The circular key element of the identity refers to the function of the space as a creative hub for people from different artistic disciplines, the generous amount of white space indicates contextual exploration, and the stenciled typeface stands for the artistic process and spontaneous workflow of a growing interdisciplinary community.

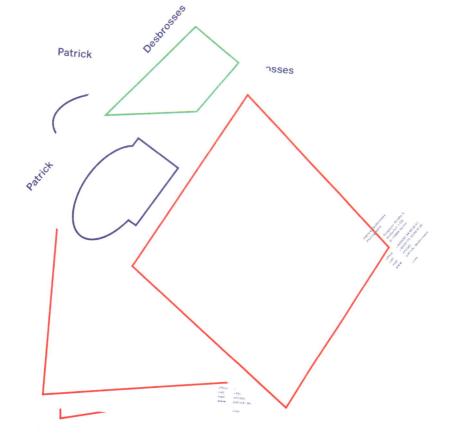

Patrick Desbrosses

Berlin, Germany

HelloMe, 2011

Patrick Desbrosses is a photographer. His intimate portraits, fashion shots, and photo stories are playful interpretations of reality. HelloMe created a modular and equally playful identity system based on the use of individual colored frames. The basic colors red, blue, and green follow the color mode of digital photography. The stationery is printed on a three-color Risograph copier, and each business card is individually hand-stamped by Patrick to underline the photographer's very personal approach. A set of flyers, posters and a 48-page catalogue, each including a signed and numbered original photo print, accompanies Patrick Desbrosses' Berlin solo exhibition "Es sind die kleinen Dinge die töten" (It's the little things that kill).

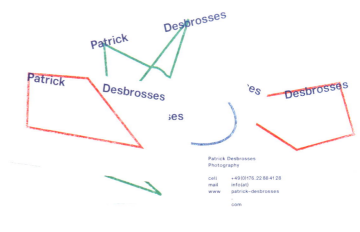

Upii
Cupcakes

Rio de Janeiro, Brazil

Rejane Dal Bello, 2011

Since it was founded in 2009, Upii cupcakes have gained a good reputation among party lovers and sweet-toothed consumers. Catering for a wide range of events from children's birthday parties to weddings, celebration has always been the central theme. Rejane Dal Bello translated this into a visual corporate language consisting of super vivid spot colors, and bold and playful type. Adhesive label sheets provide a diverse set of branding devices in various tones and shapes to be stuck onto cake wrapping paper, bags, and other materials.

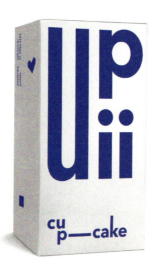

Patter & Mustique

Valencia, Spain

Rocío Martinavarro, 2011

Patter & Mustique is a swimwear brand that will launch its first collection in Spring-Summer 2012. Commissioned with the visual representation of the new brand, Rocío Martinavarro created a fairly traditional maritime aesthetic. One of the key elements of Patter & Mustique's graphic identity is an ampersand in the shape of a nautical eight knot; a wavy pattern supports the overall maritime feel. Typical for its use in traditional trademarks, the ampersand conveys the idea of alliance, which is played on by the variety of word combinations used throughout the brand identity: Rock & Roll, Fish & Chips, Beach & Pool.

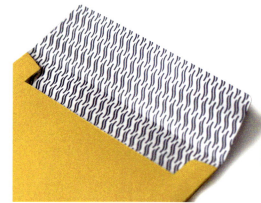

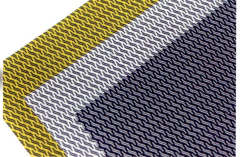

Marmalade Toast

Singapore, Singapore

And Larry, 2010

The upmarket gourmet café used to be called just "Toast." Its new name, "Marmalade Toast," refers to its parent company, The Marmalade Group. And Larry tweaked the brand mark visually: The letters of the word toast look as if they have just popped out of a toaster, and the bottom edge of the letters look slightly melted.

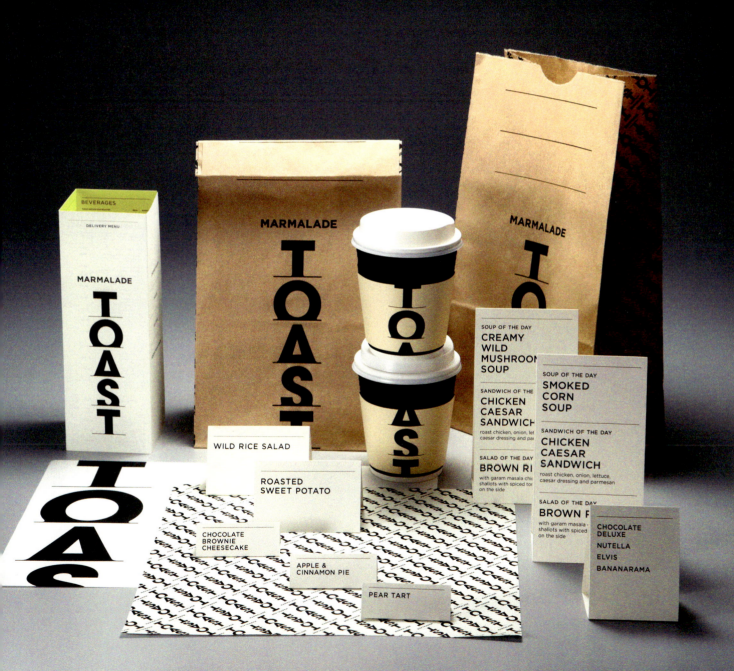

Joe and Co.

London, UK

Hyperkit, 2010

Joe Mills is a man with a passion for men's hairdressing. Fulfilling his dream of a male grooming space and gentlemen's barbershop with a contemporary twist, he opened Joe and Co. in 2010. Tucked away on a popular back street in Soho, Joe and his team deliver impressive haircuts in an unconventional setting. Responding to Joe's rejection of his trade's rather stiff tradition, Hyperkit deconstructed the conventional barbershop situation and rebuilt it for a contemporary audience. Inspired by the arrangement of tools in workshops, sheds, and garages, they developed a straightforward and functional aesthetic based on diverse combinations of materials and textures. Elements like the geometric logo or the black-and-white checked lino floors form a deliberate contrast to the ornamental emblems and patterns typically found in barbershops.

Cobbler Caballero

Sydney, Australia

Stewart Hollenstein, 2010

Founded and run by Andres Miranda and his family, Cobbler Caballero is dedicated to the repair of shoes, watches, and leather goods. A familiy of Chilean fine craftsmen, the Mirandas wanted their cultural background reflected in the brand and store identity and commissioned Felicity Stewart and Matthias Hollenstein of Stewart Hollenstein to develop a corresponding visual language.

A *caballero* is a Spanish gentleman, a cavalier. The logo—a unique, playful lettering—is based on the manual manipulation of a shoelace. The shop is conceived as an open workshop with no walls seperating cobbler and customer. It is framed by a "shoe library"—a continuous wall of plywood shelving that wraps around the narrow shops wall, allowing for the organization and display of shoes and products. The dark ceiling, floor, and walls recede, bringing the craft, texture, and machinery of the cobbling process focus.

Much of the building fabric of the shop's previous tenant was restored and given a new lease of life.

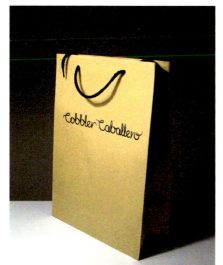

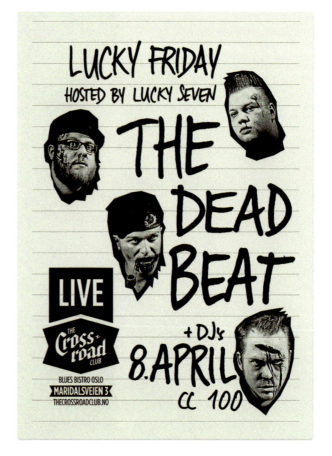

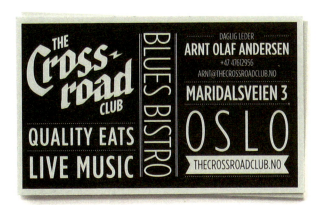

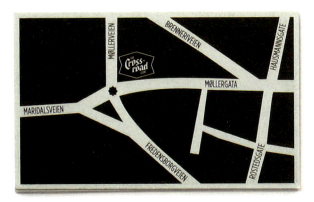

Cross
Road Club

Oslo, Norway

The Metric System, 2011

Located in Oslo's party district Grünerløkka, the Cross Road Club offers drinks, a limited but fine selection of food and—most notably—live music by both international and local blues artists. Aware that blues culture has a lot more to it than generally assumed, the Cross Road Club covers a variety of facets of the genre.

Picking up on the club's intention, The Metric System developed a brand language beyond the genre's visual clichés. Music graphics are just one source of inspiration; a Robert Johnson record, *The Crossroad Blues,* set the style for the typography. Vintage beer labels and the visual characteristics of the biker community served as additional cues for the designers.

Sita Murt

Barcelona, Spain

Clase BCN, 2006

"Sita Murt's corporate identity reflects the label's approach to fashion: simplicity, timelessness, and creativity."

Sita Murt is a Catalan fashion designer and businesswoman, whose fast-expanding women's label developed out of Esteve Aguilera, a leading family-owned knitwear producer with a long tradition in the textiles industry. Entrusted with the task of translating the key aspects of Sita's collection into a corporate visual language, Clase BCN focused on the contrast between subtle minimalism and sharp experimentation. They developed a simple but distinct logotype accompanied by a disorderly line as an element for versatile application.

The basic black-and-white identity was followed by flashy variations developed to represent Sita Murt's popup stores. The first one opened in Sitges in summer 2010 and impressed customers with shrill hand-painted wall graphics in fluorescent ink. In addition to the interior, Clase BCN produced a set of exclusively branded materials such as hand-painted sketchbooks, stationery, labels, and flyers for the temporary sales venue.

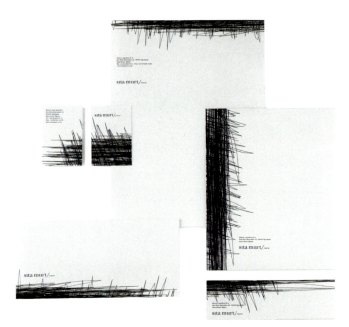

AZITA

Frankfurt, Germany

**Aoki & Matsumoto,
2009 (ongoing)**

Azita is a select clothing store in Frankfurt. Founded in 2005 as a skate shop, the small business developed over the years—not in size, but in shifting its focus from sneakers and streetwear to fashion.

It grew up with its client base, and Aoki & Matsumoto refined its visual identity accordingly. But while the visual elements and typographic subtleties keep on being adjusted, the original logo and font remain unchanged to reflect Azita's roots in '90s skateboard culture.

MUSGRAVE RITUAL

Azıta GmbH, Münzgasse 10, 60311 Frankfurt
contact@azitastore.com, +49 69 219 79 644
http://www.azitastore.com

FIVE ORANGE PIPS

Azıta GmbH, Münzgasse 10, 60311 Frankfurt
contact@azitastore.com, +49 69 219 79 644
http://www.azitastore.com

NAVAL TREATY

Azıta GmbH, Münzgasse 10, 60311 Frankfurt
contact@azitastore.com, +49 69 219 79 644
http://www.azitastore.com

2009

GOD BLESS AZITA

Azıta GmbH, Münzgasse 10, 60311 Frankfurt
contact@azitastore.com, +49 69 219 79 644
http://www.azitastore.com
Montag bis Samstag 11:00 — 19:00

POP UP © MMIX

GOETHEPLATZ 9, 60311 FRANKFURT
BIS 04.01.2010 TÄGLICH 10:00 — 19:00

SONNTAG 20.12. 13:00 — 18:00
SAMSTAG 24.12. 10:00 — 14:00
SAMSTAG 31.12. 10:00 — 14:00

ACNE STUDIOS, AIRBAG CRAFTWORKS,
A.P.C., BLESS, COMME DES GARÇONS,
FABRIC INTER-SEASON, HENRIK VIBSKOV,
OPENING CEREMONY, RAF BY RAF SIMONS,
REALITY STUDIO, SASKIA DIEZ, WOODWOOD

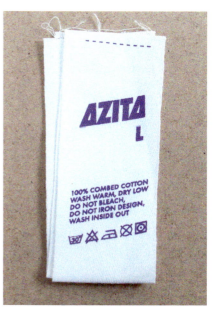

AZITA
L

100% COMBED COTTON
WASH WARM, DRY LOW
DO NOT BLEACH,
DO NOT IRON DESIGN,
WASH INSIDE OUT

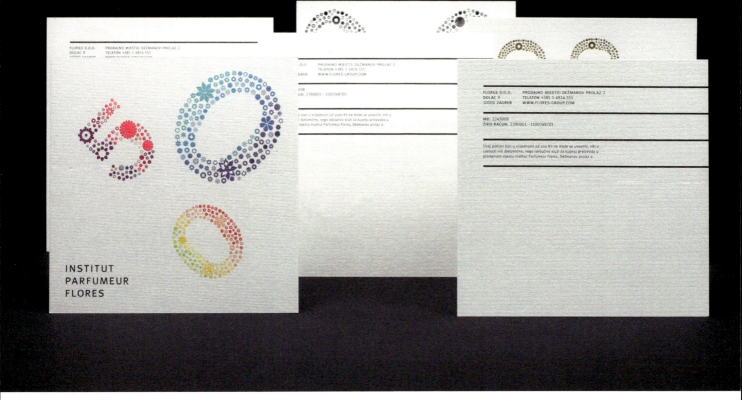

Institut Parfumeur Flores

Zagreb, Croatia

Bunch, 2009

Institut Parfumeur Flores is a small niche perfumery founded by the perfume experts at Teo Cabanel. Hidden in the byroads of Zagreb, it offers a wide range of fragrances and cosmetics, along with pastries and coffee in its own small café.

Working with a pallet of flower illustrations, fairly conventional typography, and a lot of white space, Bunch developed a brand identity that is playfully diverse and elegant at the same time. The branding includes signage, bags, stickers, pencils, ribbons, and labels along with various promotional applications for both the interior and exterior of the store.

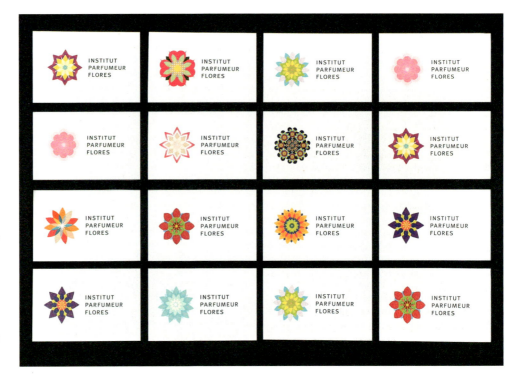

"Working with Bunch was a unique experience for us, bringing a high end concept of luxury retail from the international point of view to a challenging Croatian market."

Sunny Side Up

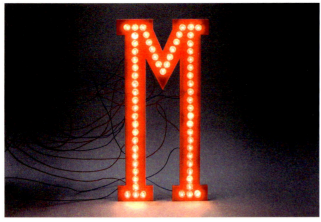

Marawa the Amazing

London, UK

Mind Design, 2010

Marawa is a renowned performer and acrobat, whose signature hoola hooping style is recognized internationally, both live and on various music videos and TV shows. Hoola hoop is her specialty, but she also does jump roping, rollerskating, and trapeze acts, wowing audiences around the world. To support Marawa as a personal brand, Mind Design created a characteristic corporate image that feels like a contemporary interpretation of traditional circus and varieté aesthetics. The logotype imitates rows of light bulbs, reminiscent of those used for old-fashioned revue theater displays. The stationery is printed using three spot colors and a range of different illustrations, suggesting Marawa's unique style and artistic versatility.

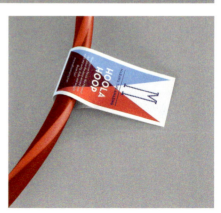

Playlab

London, UK

Mind Design, 2009

Identity and stationery for Playlab, a workshop space or creative playground for stressed adults. True to their tagline "The Imagination Gym," Playlab aims to add fun and vitality to communications, education, entertainment, and events.

Mind Design developed a corporate image for Playlab. Focusing on the mixture of pleasure and vigor, they created a seemingly random mix of textbook illustrations and fun graphic symbols. The stationery is printed in fluorescent spot colors with the actual logo blind embossed. Details are filled in using a rubber stamp.

Munt la Reita

Cimalmotto, Switzerland

Pirol, 2009

Munt la Reita is an organic farm with the mission of protecting the natural environment and living in harmony with it. Located in the mountains in the south of Switzerland, the farm is run as a family business by Verena and Markus Senn, who offer holidays in a selection of cosy cottages and flats, and sell a fine selection of organic products such as cheese, salametti, and fresh garden vegetables in their tiny shop.

The corporate identity by Pirol focuses on Munt la Reita's real protagonists: the farm animals. Using snapshots taken by the farmers themselves, the designers created a series of promotional postcards, a tourist information leaflet, and labels for the farm products.

REASSEMBLING

REFLECTION

TANGIBLE

Buitenwerk-plaats

Starnmeer, Netherlands

Cobbenhagen Hendriksen, 2010

Buitenwerkplaats Amsterdam is a refurbished farm situated in the countryside of Noord-Holland, half an hour from Amsterdam. It rents out reasonably priced workspaces in an inspirational setting, surrounded by the typically Dutch flat landscape, fresh air, and orchard and vegetable gardens. With the objective of enhancing creative processes and boosting concentration levels, Buitenwerkplaats offers its guests a refreshing change of scene. Cobbenhagen Hendriksen designed postcards, the website, and advertisements for the non-profit organization. A group of illustrations references Buitenwerkplaats's core values. Blue skies and green trees symbolize nature, black type the intellectual work stimulated by it. Printed on sticker sheets, the visual elements make a flexible set of low-cost branding devices.

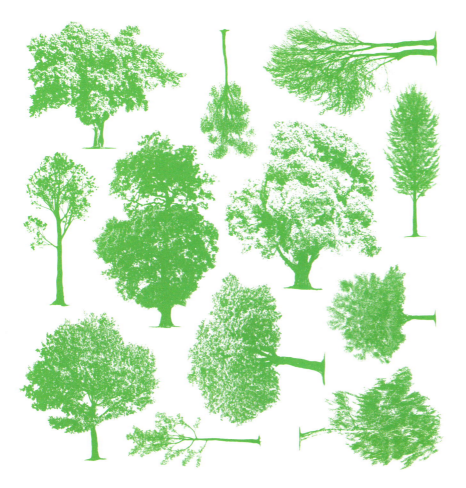

IDEOLOGY EVOLVING CORE
ARCHETYPICAL DEVOTION
ELABORATION AUTHENTICITY
COMPREHENSION FRAME
RESULTS FLOW CONTEXT
EPIPHANY OBSERVATIONS
IN-SEARCH-OF PRINCIPLES
VARIATION IDEAS QUALITY
DEFINING FRAMEWORK
REASSEMBLING IMAGINARY

BUITENWERKPLAATS ~~AMSTERDAM~~
STARNMEERDIJK 6
1488 AG STARNMEER

INFO@BUITENWERKPLAATS.NL
WWW.BUITENWERKPLAATS.NL

Robertson

Monterrey, Mexico

Manifiesto Futura, 2011

Robertson is a printing press offering a wide range of both traditional and rather unconventional services and techniques. To develop a distinct and memorable visual identity, Manifiesto Futura focused on Robertson's pledge to "print out of the box." Taking the tagline literally, they created a range of photographic compositions that present printing techniques in the manner of lunch offers.

Land Art Contemporary

Drenthe, Netherlands

Cobbenhagen Hendriksen, 2011

Land Art Contemporary is exactly what its name suggests: an initiative dealing with the contemporary aspects of land art. Launched in September 2011, it focuses on the presentation of art projects and cultural heritage in the rural environment of Drenthe.

Cobbenhagen Hendriksen teamed up with Radim Peško of the RP Digital Type Foundry to develop the typeface "Smiro," which serves as a key element of Land Art Contemporary's corporate identity. Inspired by the basic shape of a serif typeface and the ephemeral nature of land art, Smiro's shapes vary like shadows observed in the course of a day.

AABBCCCDDEEE
FFGGGHHHIIJJ
KKLLMMMNN
OOPPQQQRRSSS
TTUUVVWW
XXYYZZ00112233
445566778899
//*-—--—+?!i@#!

LAND ART CONTEM PORARY

www.landartcontemporary.nl

Fabbrica

Toronto, Canada

Concrete, 2010

Canadian celebrity chef and entrepreneur Mark McEwan has a new venture, the "true-to-form Italian restaurant" Fabbrica. The menu is inspired by Italian classics (roasted fish, Neapolitan pizza from wood-burning ovens, homemade pasta etc.), and so is Fabricca's visual identity: Working closely with McEwan and architects Giannone Petricone Associates, Concrete borrowed the design aesthetic of post-war Italy (Pirelli, Gio Ponti, Federico Fellini etc.). Rich colors and strong geometric shapes are contrasted with industrial principles (Fabbrica is the Italian word for "factory"), shaping up as a contemporary interpretation of iconic Italian style.

Tess
Management

London, UK

Mind Design, 2009

The name Tess Management is based on the initials of Tori Edwards and Sian Steel, who founded the model agency in 2009 to replace their former business Independent Models. Based in London, Tess represents a huge range of models, both new faces and well-established names like Naomi Campbell and Erin O'Connor.

Playing on the variety of Tess's models and clients, Mind Design created a corporate identity that uses several logo variations based on a modular system of art deco inspired ornamental battens and vignettes. The same elements are used to overlap the images of the models on various printed applications and on the website, making them look like abstract versions of traditionally framed portraits.

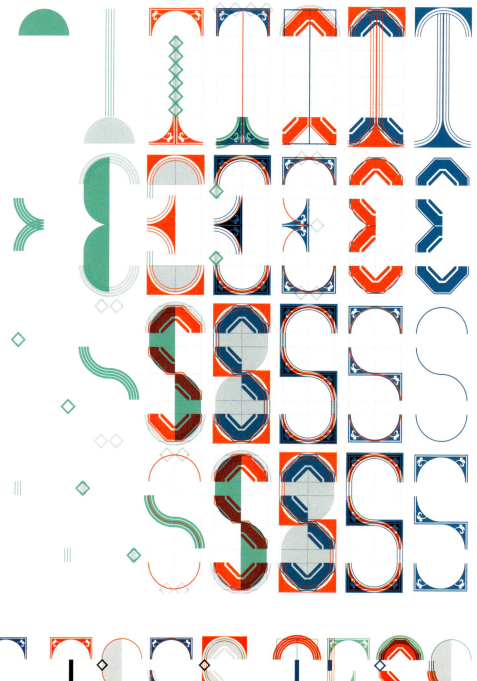

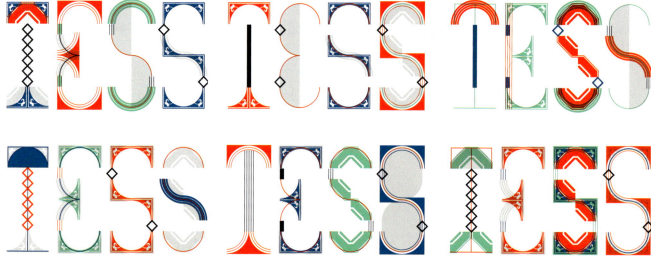

NAOMI CAMPBELL

ZOMBIE
SICKNESS
AND
PREGNA
BITC

...m as
...nsborgveien N° 3...
Oslo

«ZOMBIE SICKNESS AND PREGNANT BITCHES» VISES PÅ PARKTEATER
26.JANUAR.2011 — KL.20.00. CC. 50,-

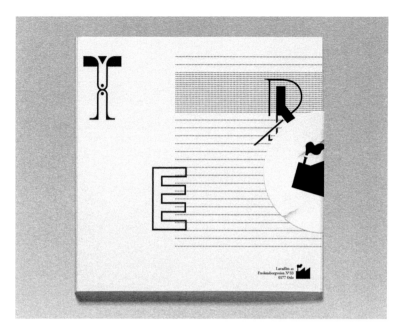

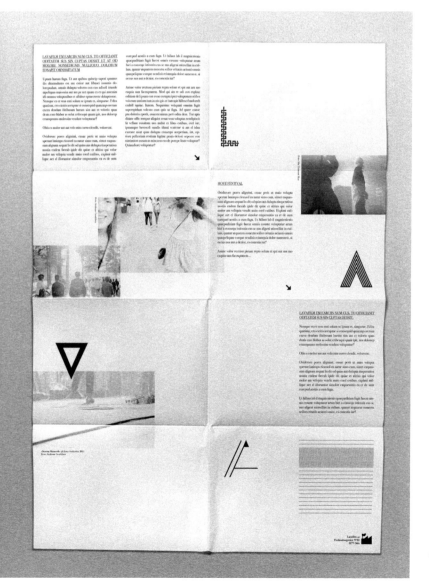

PAGES 50–53

Lavafilm

Oslo, Norway

Bureau Bruneau, 2011

Lavafilm is the collaborative project of the two Norwegian filmmakers Ida Thurmann-Moe and Andreas Grødtlien. In their studio in Oslo they produce and direct music videos, commercials, and short films, mainly within the fashion, design, and advertising industries. To pique the interest of Lavafilm's creative clientele, Bureau Bruneau designed a unique and highly versatile brand identity, based on a variety of custom letterforms that can be used in infinite combinations.

53

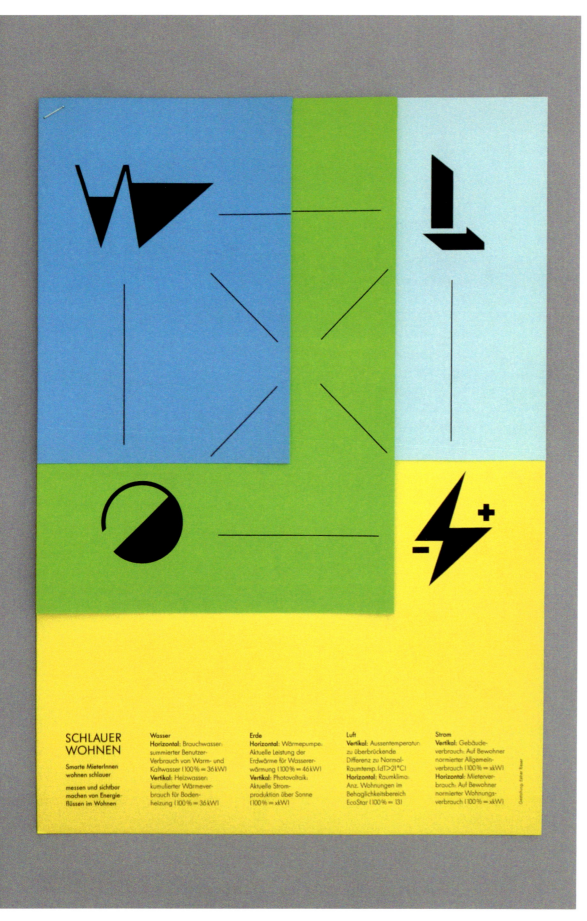

Schlauer Wohnen

Zurich, Switzerland

Esther Rieser, 2011

Anja Meyer and Urs Hugentobler are researchers. Their "2000-watt society" project Schlauer Wohnen (smarter living) monitors and displays the use of energy in multifamily-housing.

Esther Rieser's identity for the project visualizes the four kinds of resources used in the house, and introduces four symbols that are based on the shape of their first letters: water, earth, air, and electricity (German: Wasser, Erde, Luft, Strom). Connected by fine diagonal lines, they work as an overall brand visual that reflects the shape of the square display installed in the clients' hallways.

TenOverSix

New York City, USA

"We want the experience at TenOverSix to be one of discovery, and we want it to be fun."

TenOverSix is a boutique and gallery-like installation space in Los Angeles offering high-concept designer accessories. The boutique's name comes from the price tag "10/6" (10 pounds 6 shillings) on the Mad Hatter's hat in *Alice in Wonderland*. Its corporate image by RoAndCo Studio draws on the vernacular of contemporary price tags.

Shopping at TenOverSix is intended to be fun. To introduce this mission to the visual representation of the brand, RoAndCo Studio borrowed the color palette from Monopoly money, and re-purposed gold "discount" stickers as the brand's signature symbol.

PAGE 57

Kapulica

Zagreb, Croatia

Bunch, 2007

The creative events agency Kapulica was established in 2007 by Kresimir Tadija Kapulica. With a degree in Fine Arts and a background in Art Direction, Kresimir focuses on the creative side of event marketing.

Working for clients from various fields, Kapulica needed a visual identity to bridge the gap between artistic ambition and strict business interests. Bunch used the letter K as the key visual to express the creative mindset of the studio. Designing dozens of different Ks to be applied to specific applications across the identity, they created a brand identity that is artistically ambitious and colorful, without compromising on a reliable, serious feel. The letterhead is kept simple and official with a varnished K. The black K on the business cards can be popped open to reveal an illustrated K beneath.

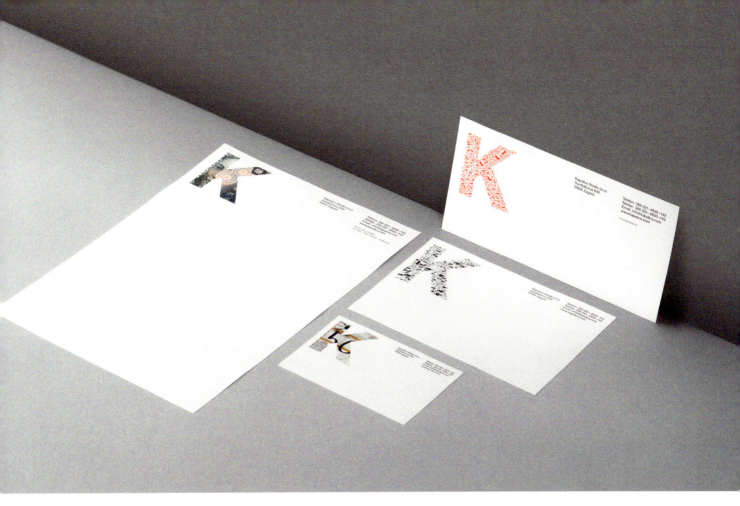

D100
Dentistry

London, UK

Mind Design, 2009

"We've always wanted to create a dental practice that is as much a place to relax and linger as it is a place for excellent dentistry."

D100 is the implementation of Dr. Andrew Parkman's vision of a dental practice that patients look forward to visiting. Located within the Barbican residential estate, the modern practice offers high-performance dentistry and a very personal service in a relaxed, friendly environment. The practice identity by Mind Design supports Parkman's notion of a pleasant customer experience. Aiming to ease the fear of going to the dentist, the designers drew inspiration from the raking patterns around stones in Japanese Zen gardens. Harmonious shapes decorate the practice's accessories and furniture, like protective enamel layers around teeth or ring-of-confidence halos around the customers' frayed nerves.

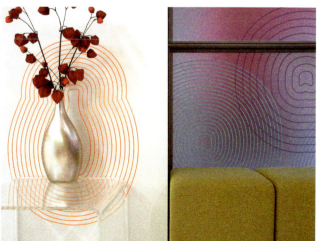

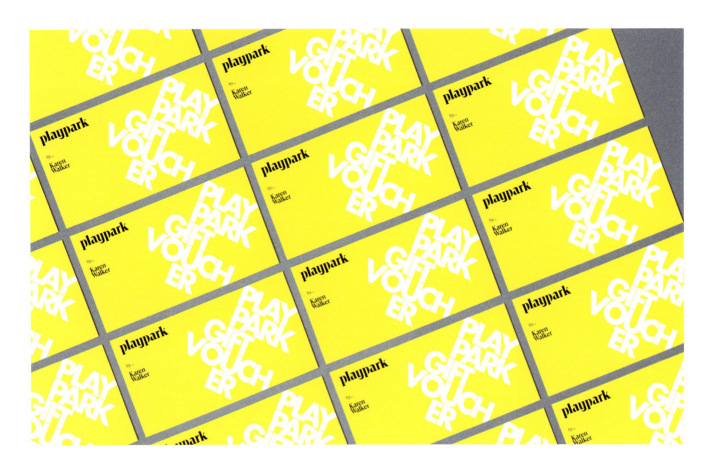

Playpark

Auckland, New Zealand

Brogen Averill, 2011

Karen Walker is a fashion designer and the Auckland-based
fashion concept store Playpark
is one of her many ventures.
Conceived of as a space to sell
high-end fashion in a gallery-like
context, the brand called for a
sophisticated corporate aesthetic. Brogen Averill's answer
is simple and minimal, yellow,
white, and black. The Playpark
lettering forms the basis of the
corporate identity, a yellow and
white neon tube is its striking
highlight. Used as in-store decoration and on image photos, the
readymade key visual propa-
gates a degree of spiritual kin-
ship to the art world.

playpark

playpark

by...

Karen
Walker

Sunny Side Up

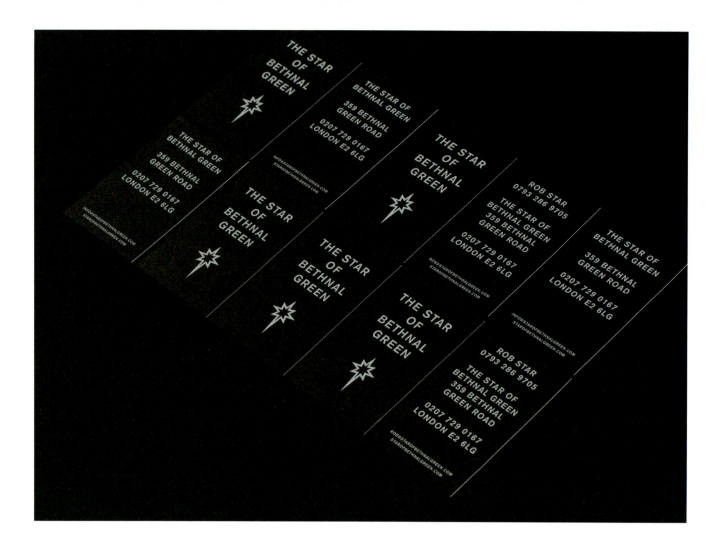

Star of
Bethnal
Green
and Star
of Kings

London, UK

Bunch, 2008 and 2011

A decade of club and venue promoting experience forms the basis of Rob Star entrepreneurial ventures: The Star of Bethnal Green is a pub and restaurant in East London, and Star of Kings is its little sister in North London. Commissioned with the branding of the two venues, Bunch developed a key symbol of a long-tailed star to pop up almost everywhere, from the pubs' printed materials, the pint glasses, or on custom-made wallpaper. In 2010, a Bunch of Stars exhibition was put on, for which illustrators from around the world were asked to interpret the venue's key branding element in their own style. To distinguish the Star of Kings from its older sister, it comes with a K within its stars and a range of single color illustrations of a king.

"Having taken a failing East End gig venue and made it one of London's essential whatever-the-occasion venues—The Star of Bethnal Green—Rob Star has set himself a new challenge. The co-founder of the legendary mulletover parties is driving ahead of the King's Cross Central pack, and opening a venue that will be the pride of the new city."

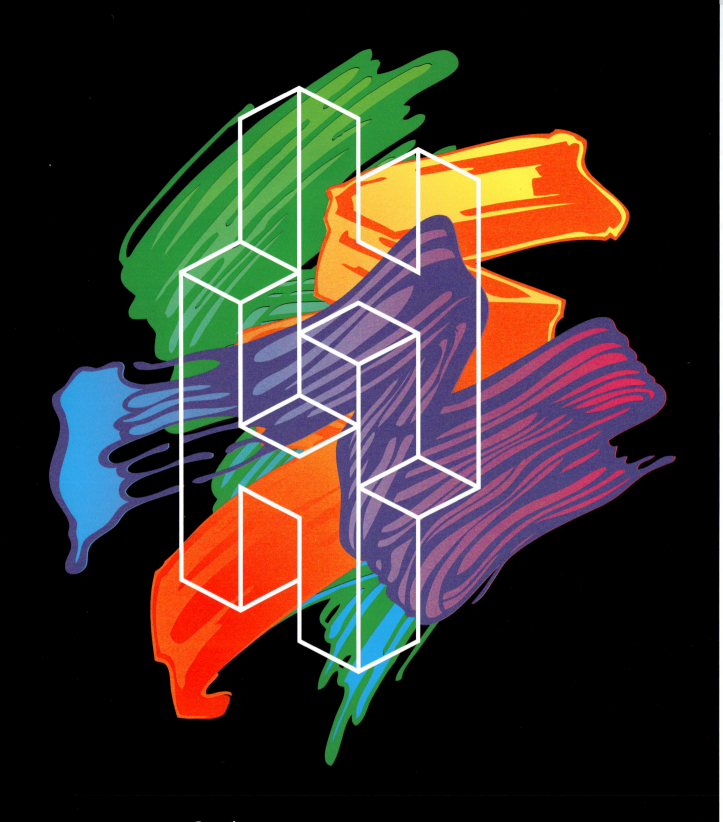

Henhouse ®

POST PRODUCTION

SPRING HOUSE 10 SPRING PLACE LONDON NW5 3BH T +44 (0)20 7428 7171 F +44 (0)20 7428 7181 WWW.HENHOUSEMEDIA.CO.UK

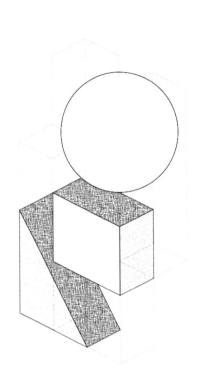

Henhouse

POST PRODUCTION

SPRING HOUSE 10 SPRING PLACE LONDON NW5 3BH
T +44 (0)20 7428 7171 F +44 (0)20 7428 7181
WWW.HENHOUSEMEDIA.CO.UK

Henhouse

London, UK

Andreas Neophytou, 2007

Henhouse is a London-based post-production company specializing in luxury and fashion media.

Asked to develop their corporate image, Andreas Neophytou designed an "HH" logomark for Henhouse that plays with the concept of optical illusion—a reference to the studio's extensive skill base in the field of image manipulation and the corresponding ability to present the impossible as visual reality. Using the HH logo mark as a grid, the designer created a set of accompanying brand icons to represent the different facets and forms of media that Henhouse's work covers: film, photography, CGI, and digital imagery.

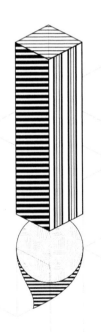

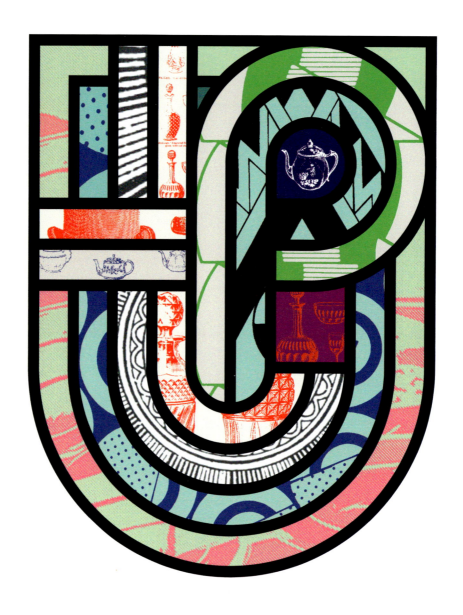

THE
PHENE

LILY BOURNE
Managing Director

+44(0)7738 456 133 +44(0)20 7352 3372
9 Phene St. Chelsea, London SW3 5NY
lily.bourne@thephene.com
www.thephene.com

BEAUTY   FASHION   HOME   DELI

THE
PHENE

The Phene

London, UK

<u>Andreas Neophytou</u>, 2009

The Phene is a restaurant, deli, and boutique at 9 Phene St in Chelsea, London. The building used to house The Phene Arms, a notorious drinking den much loved by celebrities such as George Best and Oliver Reed. The new owner, Lily Bourne, the 24-year-old daughter of two millionaires, fitted it to meet the needs and tastes of the local gilded youth and commissioned Andreas Neophytou with the development of an appropriate brand identity.

The designer came up with a clever mix of traditional and poppy elements. The shield symbol of the logo is a nod to the history of the premises. The many patterned bands making up the monogram T.P. represent the variety of lifestyle consumables on offer: from food over fashion (Lily sells her own fashion range "Lily London" upstairs) to household goods.

Le Petit Bain

Paris, France

Lola Duval, 2011

UNE ÎLE DANS LA VILLE CONCERTS RESTAURANT ATELIERS EXPOS

EST OUVERT À TOUS

PETIT BAIN

Still in the early stages of its development, Le Petit Bain aims to become a buzzing cultural hub. Lying at anchor in Port de la Gare (Paris 13°), it serves as a floating home for a musical venue, a musical and multimedia creation studio, a restaurant, a web radio and a planted terrace. As a creative laboratory, Le Petit Bain welcomes artists from various disciplines to exhibit and discuss their work. As a social welfare organization it aims to support the long-term unemployed or ex-convicts in their search for a new job. As an architectural project in itself it is led by the visionary architects' collective Encore Heureux. As a corporate identity project it was entrusted to Lola Duval, who focused on clarity to establish a calm backdrop for a mixed agenda and the resulting broad range of topical promotion material.

EN FAIRE TOUT UN FROMAGE

CHEZ PETIT BAIN, MON CONTACT C'EST :

WWW.PETITBAIN.ORG

☐ **RICARDO ESTEBAN**
DIRECTION
ricardo@petitbain.org

☐ **ANTOINE THIBAULT**
ADMINISTRATION
antoine@petitbain.org

☐ **PRISCILLE BARON**
MÉDIATION, ACTION CULTURELLE
priscille@petitbain.org

☐ **CLAIRE CHEMINEAU**
MÉDIATION, ACTION CULTURELLE
claire@petitbain.org

☐ **LAURA SCOT**
PROGRAMMATION
laura@petitbain.org

☐ **DELPHINE ZEHNDER**
COMMUNICATION, RELATIONS PRESSE
delphine@petitbain.org

☐ **FABRICE BOY**
PROJET INSERTION PAR L'ÉCONOMIE
fabrice@petitbain.org

PETIT BAIN

PENSER BIEN

ET CRIER, CRIER-ER : «ALINE!»

LA TERRASSE DE PETIT BAIN MODE D'EMPLOI JUILLET 2010

Envolés les ballons qui cachaient le soleil… Revoilà l'été pour notre île dans la ville. Un grand merci à celles et ceux qui sont venus au bord de l'eau assister en direct à nos réglages et autres balbutiements. Cette aventure ne fait que commencer et bien que ce quai soit notre bac à sable depuis longtemps, y revenir a des allures de premiers pas.

Petit Bain est un équipement culturel flottant et une entreprise d'insertion qui viendra s'amarrer sur la Seine au printemps 2011. Un espace pour écouter, voir, danser, manger, goûter… Un lieu de vie dans le 13e arrondissement pour montrer qu'il est possible d'entreprendre autrement.

En partenariat avec la piscine Joséphine Baker

MAIRIE DE PARIS
❋ île deFrance
TRUFFAUT
À NOUS
90bpm.com
TROIS

de 12h à 15h et de 18h à 22h le dimanche restauration en continu de 11h à 20h fermé le lundi

SAMEDI 3 JUILLET

DE 19 H 30 À 21 H 30
DANS MON JUKE-BOX avec *Rémy Kolpa Kopoul* (FR / Elektropik)

DIMANCHE 4 JUILLET
DE 15 H 30 À 18 H 30
LA LENTEUR avec *Isabelle Brunaud* (atelier + bal jam, 10 €, tout public)

MARDI 6 JUIL. | JEUDI 8 JUIL. | VENDREDI 9 JUIL.
DE 19 H À 19 H 30
COMMENT CASSER UNE BOUTEILLE SUR DU SABLE, Lecture par *Frédéric Danos*

SAMEDI 10 JUILLET
DE 19 H 30 À 21 H 30
DANS MON JUKE-BOX avec *Blackjoy* (FR / électro libre)

DIMANCHE 11 JUILLET
DE 15 H 30 À 18 H 30
LA MARCHE avec *Edwine Fournier* (atelier + bal jam, 10 €, tout public)

MARDI 13 JUILLET
À 18 H
LA MARCHE, LA LENTEUR, LE SAUVAGE avec *E. Fournier, I. Brunaud et P. Chevalier* (atelier + bal jam, gratuit, tout public)

INTERVENTION SURPRISE du collectif *Studiobüro* (FR)

DE 20 H À 00 H
GRAND BAL TROPICAL avec CIBELLE (BR-GB / live), AXEL KRYGIER (AR-FR / live) HUGO MENDEZ (GB / dj-set) et DJ SOULIST (FR / dj-set)

DE 23 H À 05 H
TRECK POÉTIQUE EN BORDS DE SEINE départ Terrasse, avec *Denis Moreau* (5 € + Ticket RER)

JEUDI 15 JUILLET | VENDREDI 16 JUILLET
DE 19 H À 19 H 30
COMMENT CASSER UNE BOUTEILLE SUR DU SABLE, Lecture par *Frédéric Danos*

SAMEDI 17 JUILLET
DE 15 H À 17 H BAIN-DE-PIEDS-BOUTURAGE avec *Fabio Piccioli et Antoine Quenardel* (5 €, tout public)

DE 19 H 30 À 21 H 30 DANS MON JUKE-BOX avec *Luc Supra* (FR / more than super)

DIMANCHE 18 JUILLET
DE 15 H 30 À 18 H 30
LA MARCHE avec *Edwine Fournier* (atelier + bal jam, 10 €, tout public)

SAMEDI 24 JUILLET
DE 17 H À 22 H FÊTE BELGE avec LEFTO (dj-set), JAMES DEANO (stand-up), THE GARDENING GROUP (live) …

À 22 H IL ÉTAIT UNE FRITE UNE FOIS de *Pierre-Olivier François*

DIMANCHE 25 JUILLET
DE 15 H 30 À 18 H 30
LA LENTEUR avec *Isabelle Brunaud* (atelier + bal jam, 10 €, tout public)

DE 17 H À 22 H FÊTE BELGE avec JEAN MIKILI (live) LE TON MITE (live)

MERCREDI 28 JUILLET
DE 15 H À 17 H SUCCULENTES AQUATIQUES avec *Camille Barberi* (5 €, tout public)

SAMEDI 31 JUILLET
À 15 H
SAFARI BOTANIQUE départ Terrasse, avec *François Wattelier*

DE 19 H 30 À 21 H 30 DANS MON JUKE-BOX avec *Nick V* (FR / soul futuriste)

Une île dans la ville, à Paris,
dans le 13e arrondissement, au pied de la BnF, Quai François Mauriac sur le Port de la gare, devant la piscine Joséphine Baker…
M° 6 : Quai de la gare
M° 14 : Bibliothèque François Mitterrand

Horaires
du mardi au jeudi de 12h à 23h vendredi et samedi de 12h à 00h et dimanche de 11 h à 20 h

 Restauration
Petites portions ou grandes assiettes, des plats à composer et surtout à partager, midi et soir, des classiques assaisonnés d'originalité.

 Balades
Jardins, immeubles, rues… de jour comme de nuit, un Paris insolite dévoilé par des promeneurs confirmés.

Extravagances végétales
Ateliers, commandos, performances à base de chlorophylle. Le végétal envisagé comme le meilleur des villes par des paysagistes et des plasticiens.

 Ateliers danse
Mouvement ludique autour des danses à deux et de l'improvisation.

 Aux platines
Pépites et autres préciosités affinées par Dj Soulist et ses invités.

 Concerts
La nouvelle vague tropicale, pop, expérimentale.

 Séances d'écoute
Cartes blanches en création sonore et radiophonique.

 Projections
Films, documentaires, OVNI…

POUR TOUTES INFORMATIONS SUPPLÉMENTAIRES WWW.PETITBAIN.ORG

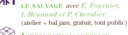

Pret·
ty
Str·
aight

At first glance, less costs less. According to the cliché, less is more. Both can be true. There is no doubt, however, that a straight and simple style in branding is not about being simple-minded or stingy.

Simplicity transmits the idea of freedom and essentiality. In the context of corporate identity and branding, that can mean not only stripped down aesthetics, but also a concise, unmistakable concept that brings out the business's most fundamental features, its core values, so to speak. The examples gathered in this section are diverse and exemplify various kinds and effects of reductionist approaches to branding.

Often interpreted as a reaction against over-designed branding, the kind that blindly follows current trends and becomes passé a year later, the keeping-it-simple aesthetic is also a way of ensuring that the visual language does not get in the way of the actual product or service on offer. The Bear Cave do without decorative elements to bring the spectacle range in Warby Parker's ✦ p. 104 shelves to the fore. Anagrama's minimal labels for fashion designer Maria Vogel ✦ p. 136 support her collection without distracting from the actual product.

Reduced aesthetics speak to those who feel overwhelmed by information overload. Candid visual translations of the business's core values give reassurance to those baffled by the multitude of double-tongued brand promises and advertising slogans the modern consumer is confronted with day by day.

Every concise translation is based on a firm understanding of its subject. Bunch's identity for Allegheny Financial, ✦ p. 146 for example, focuses on the contrast between bold and fine strokes of the typeface:

Stability is certainly key in the financial business, but the readiness to assume risk and meticulous attention to detail are crucial, too. Goodmorning Technology's corporate image for Copenhagen Parts ✦ p. 106 is based on the deliberate omission of letters, because Copenhagen Parts produce and assemble bicycle accessories to be mounted onto the customer's bike. Mind Design's custom typeface for Belmacz ✦ p. 140 adapts the coarse shapes of the raw minerals and crushed pearls that the brand's jewelry and beauty preparations are made of.

Looking at RoAndCo's branding for the fashion label Honor, ✦ p. 92 it becomes clear that stripped down branding strategies do not necessarily appear meager, but can also shape up as quite the opposite, namely as luxury and elaborate classiness. A lot of white space can be contrasted with gilded accents and toned-down flowery patterns. The result may not be minimal, but it is certainly neat, pure, and a worthwhile example in proving that not much is needed to make a brand shine.

MTLL

MTLL Arquitectos
Arquitectos Urbanismos Landscape

Luis Loya.

Lázaro Garza – Ayala 169
Tampiquito, San Pedro GG
México
CP 66240
T. + 52 (81) 8335-5661

www.mtllarquitectos.com
luis@mtllarquitectos.com

Lázaro Garza – Ayala 169
Tampiquito, San Pedro GG
México
CP 66240

www.mtllarquitectos.com
info@mtllarquitectos.com

MTLL Arquitectos
Arquitectura Construcción, Urbanismo

MTLL Arquitectos
Arquitectura Urbanismo Landscape

Lázaro Garza - Ayala 169
Tampiquito San Pedro GG
Mexico
CP 66240
T + 52 (81) 8335 5661
www.mtllarquitectos.com
info@mtllarquitectos.com

MTLL
Arquitectos

San Pedro Garza García, Mexico

Anagrama, 2011

MTLL is a young architecture firm born from the merging of Miriam Torres and Luis Loya, two experienced architects with independent trajectories. In need of an identity that would represent their practical expertise and extensive architectural knowledge, they approached Anagrama. The designers came up with a typographic brand mark based on the firm's initials. Reduced to a minimum, the logo conveys the architect duo's guiding ideals of simplicity and pragmatism. The robust body of the typography with its delicate serifs visualizes security and reliability, two core competences of the architecture industry.

MTLL Arquitectos.
Arquitectura.Urbanismo.Landscape

Lázaro Garza — Ayala 169
Tampiquito, San Pedro GG
México
CP 66240

T + 52 (81) 8335 5661

www.mtllarquitectos.com
info@mtllarquitectos.com

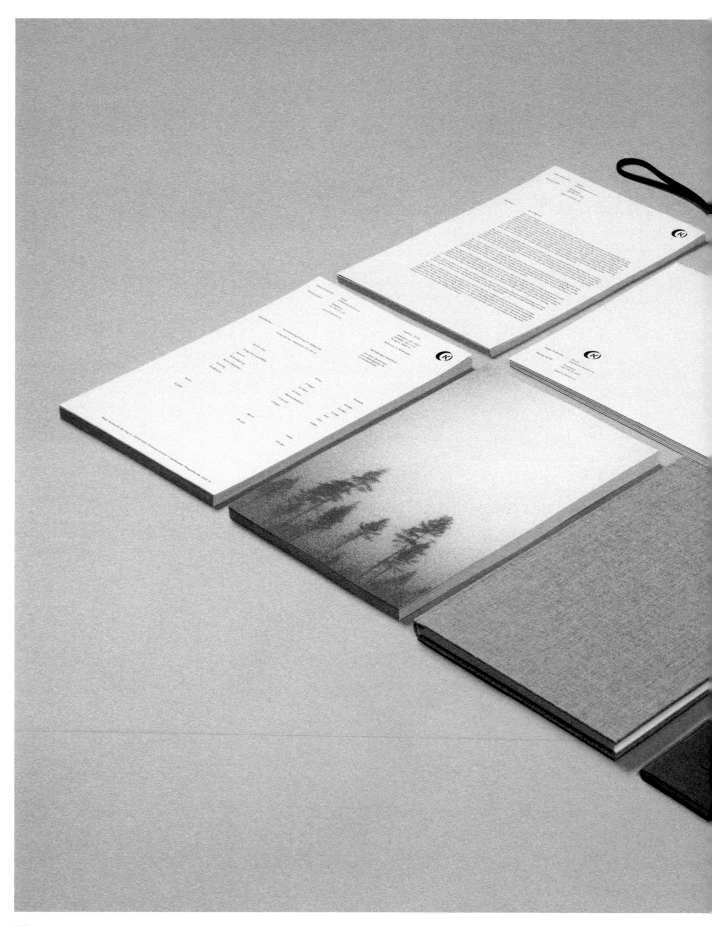

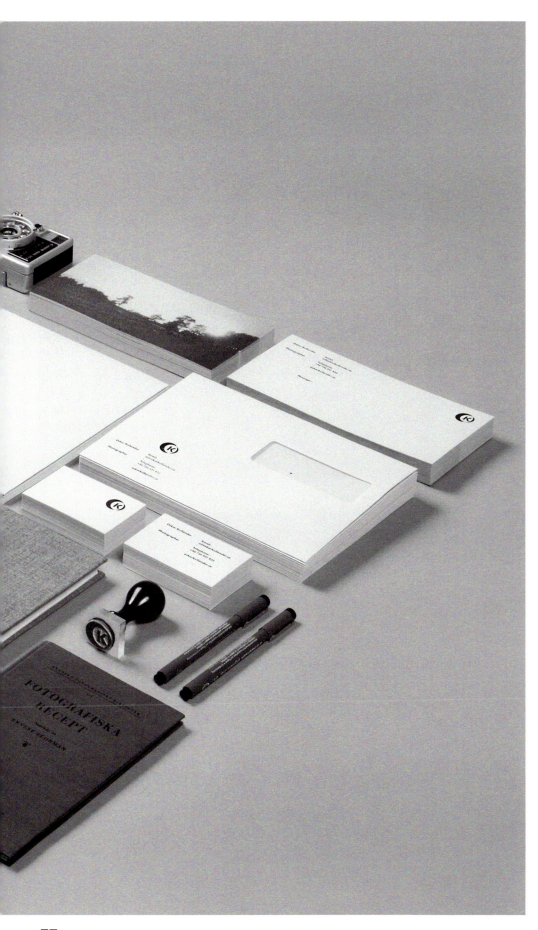

Oskar
Kullander

Stockholm, Sweden

Lundgren+Lindqvist, 2011

Oskar Kullander is a free-lance photographer based in Stockholm. Working for maga-zines, newspapers, trade press, businesses, and music videos, he has been awarded "Rookie of the Year" (2006) and won the "Swedish Picture of The Year Award" in 2007. For Kullander, Lundgren+Lindqvist created a no-nonsense identity that reflects the nature of his work without being overly descriptive. The primary element of the iden-tity is a monogram based on the photographer's initials, with the K placed within an abstracted O that looks like a camera lens.

Collin Teo
B OPTOM (UNSW)

39 Stamford Road
01-06 Stamford House
Singapore 178885

T: 65 6338 3240
F: 65 6338 5791

the.eyeplace@pacific.net.sg
www.eye-place.com

Operating Hours
Mon, Wed to Sat: 11:30am to 8pm
Sun: 11:30am to 6pm
Closed on Tues & Public Holidays

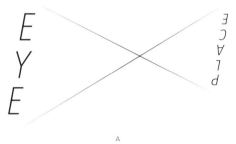

A

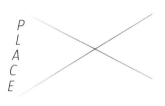

B

Eye Place

Singapore, Singapore

And Larry, 2007

Run by a bunch of optometrists with a passion for unusual spectacles, the Eye Place's shelves are filled with carefully selected designs from eyewear designers around the world. Their identity was developed by And Larry. Drawing inspiration from the workings of the human eye, the x shape of the brand mark refers to the inversion of light rays through the lens. Reverse clear foil blocking on the name card makes the brand mark shimmer on the card's surface, causing it to appear and disappear, like the projected symbols of an eye sight test.

TEL. +43·(0)·2243·22·893

TEL. +43·(0)·2243·22·893

fraxinus excelsior

TEL. +43·(0)·2243·22·893

mödling/nordhang

eremurus, bis zu 2,50m höhe im juni

TEL. +43·(0)·2243·22·893

braucht kaum wasser und ist winterhart

TEL. +43·(0)·2243·22·893

nutzfeld für gemüse und co

TEL. +43·(0)·2243·22·893

ein wieed vital auf einem wieed inmitten hochgewieed

TEL. +43·(0)·2243·22·893

...holz i mein a pejoshendi fongan...

TEL. +43·(0)·2243·22·893

250m² steinschlichtung

verdarium

DIPL.ING.MAG.ART. NORA STALZER

VERDARIUM GMBH
HAUPTSTRASSE 286 A-3411 WEIDLING
TEL. +43 (0)·2243·22 893   NORA@VERDARIUM.AT
FAX. +43 (0)·2243·34 712   WWW.VERDARIUM.AT

verdarium

verdarium

WWW.VERDARIUM.AT

RAUM FÜR GÄRTEN

Verdarium

Vienna, Austria

Moodley Brand Identity, 2009

The Verdarium is a garden concept store and planning office. It was founded in 2005 by landscape gardener Clemens Lutz and artist and architect Nora Stalzer in a small town in the middle of the Weidlinger Stiftswald near Vienna. In their 3000-square-meter "green oasis" they display a collection of weather-resistant furniture and invite their customers to enjoy the homey outdoor experience on site. Moodley Brand Identity's branding solution for the Verdarium is minimal and raw, featuring a lot of white space and logo lettering that is based on digitalized handwriting. The offbeat visual languages express the duo's rather unorthodox approach to gardening, as well as their personal notion of the garden as an individually designed home and living space.

Breitenthaler

Leibnitz, Austria

Moodley Brand Identity, 2010

For the Breitenthalers, high quality furniture design is the result of customer responsiveness, a strong creative vision, and a good understanding of construction methods. Since its beginnings in 1908, the family business "Möbelbau Breitenthaler" combines technical knowledge and craftsmanship with creative ambition and a true passion for materials, forms, and colors. The result is timeless, beautiful furniture that draws on the qualities of its fundamental material, wood.

The new corporate design by Moodley Brand Identity pays tribute to wood, celebrating its structure as a pattern and using it as the key visual throughout the identity.

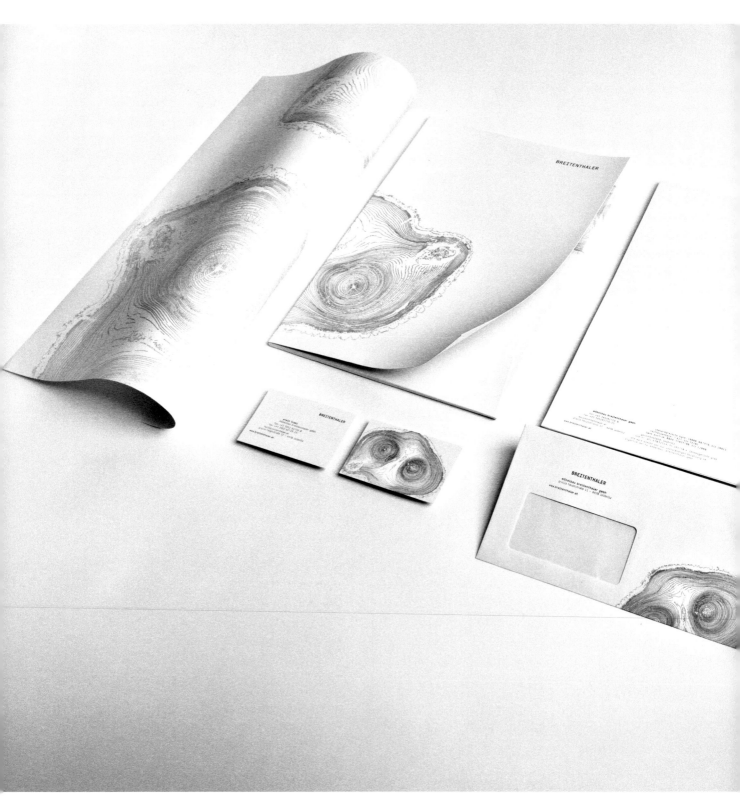

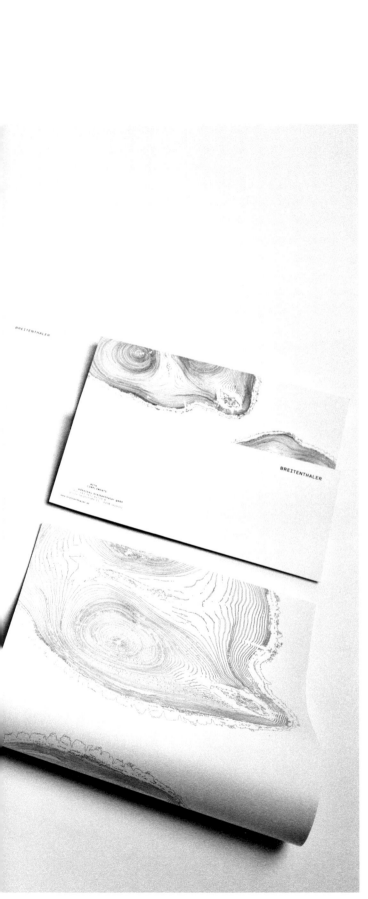

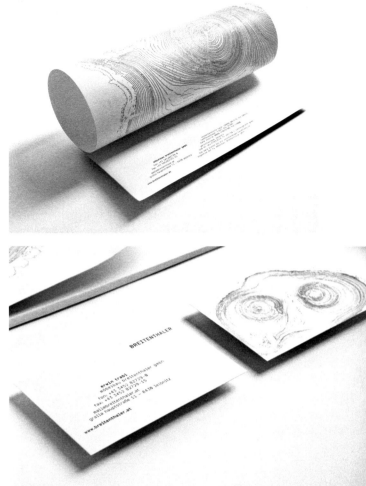

"Real good ideas for good furniture design can only be born if you take your time for the person- ality and the wishes of your clients, for your own visions and for the perfect construction of the furniture."

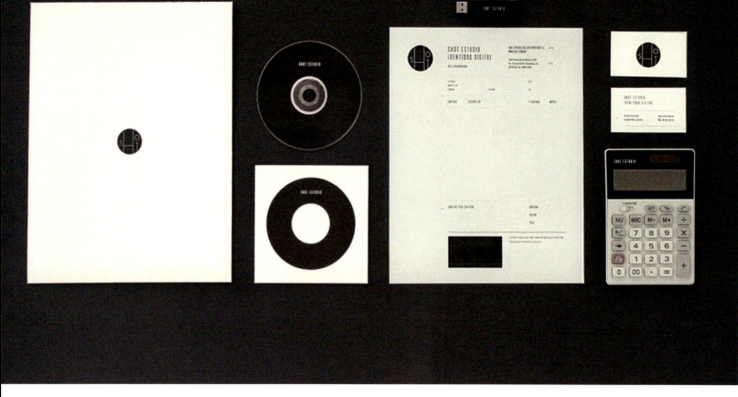

Shot
Estudio

Monterrey, Mexico

Manifiesto Futura, 2011

Shot develop digital identities. Looking for a branding solution that makes them stand out from an ever growing crowd of competitors, they asked Manifiesto Futura to develop a corporate image that would emphasize their notion of web design as subtle and sophisticated graphics. Steering clear of the visual clichés of the web design industry, the designers came up with a visual language that speaks through simplicity rather than fancy gradients and 3D effects.

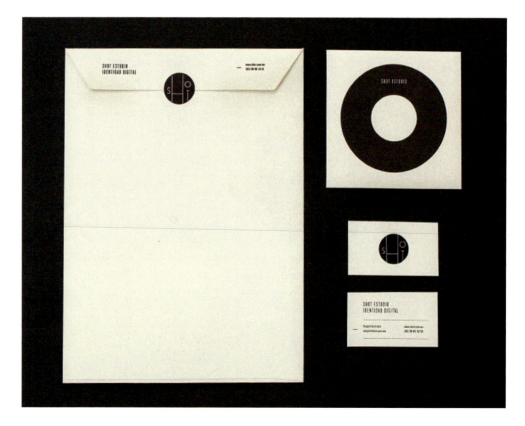

84

What
Matters Most

New York City, USA

The Bear Cave, 2011

What Matters Most is a think tank dedicated to creative film-making solutions. Approaching image-making and story-telling as craftspeople who believe in and wish to improve upon the film-making canon, What Matters Most produces both commissioned and self-initiated work with exquisite attention to detail. Trying to remain as faithful as possible to the ethos of the brand, The Bear Cave developed a corporate identity that is boldly iconic and yet clean and minimal. The logo emblem makes clever use of the company's initials, combining them to a knot-like shape that refers to What Matters Most is above all: a co-operative of artists looking to enhance each other's work through a collective process.

85

Estudio Tanguma

Monterrey, Mexico

Manifiesto Futura, 2011

Estudio Tanguma design interiors. Tanguma is not only the surname of the company's founding director, but also served as the starting point for the corporate identity by Manifiesto Futura. Inspired by the name's native American heritage, the designers created an aesthetically ambitious brand language based on repetitive geometric forms and angular patterns.

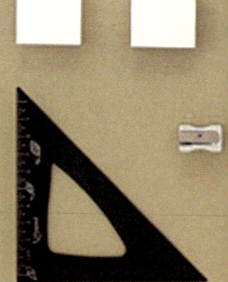

ESTUDIO
TANGUMA

BEAR RENÉ

MMVI

Bear René

Ascot, UK

Marque, 2011

Bear René are an interior design business in the south of England. With a focus on luxury home interiors, the small company needed a sophisticated brand image to reflect both their high level of craftsmanship and the loving attention to detail that is so fundamental to their work. Marque Creative's solution is based on a geometric monogram, which is in turn used as a repeat pattern and a logo mark, to be embossed, printed, stuck, or foil stamped onto both the company's communications materials and onto the range of products they sell in their studio.

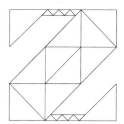

zeri crafts
زري للحرف

zeri crafts
زري للحرف

zeri crafts
زري للحرف

Zeri Crafts

Kuwait City, Kuwait

Rocío Martinavarro, 2011

The young Kuwaiti company Zeri Crafts produces handcrafted textile-based home wares and other accessories. Laila al Hamad founded the business in 2010, with modern interiors in mind and the aim of keeping the Gulf's beautiful weaving tradition alive. Since then, Zeri Crafts has been successfully developing possible new directions for an ancient tribal art form.

The visual identity by Rocío Martinavarro is a graphic interpretation of the company's product range, as much as a homage to the craft's heritage in its own right. Taking cues from *zeri,* the gold or silver thread that brightens traditional garments, and typical geometric Bedouin weaving patterns, all graphic elements are based on a modular system of golden triangles. The bilingual identity demanded a great deal of typographic attention as equal visual weight was to be given to the Latin and Arabic logotypes.

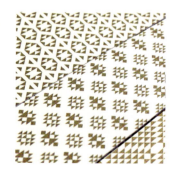

Bar Milano

New York City, USA

Established NYC, 2008

The young restaurateur Jason Denton and his brother, Joe, were already operating three successful, small-scale Italian joints in the city of New York when they opened Bar Milano, their most ambitious and conspicuously upscale venture to date. With two co-chefs, an impressively stocked wine display case, and walls covered in panels of polished marble cut from quarries in Emilia-Romagna, the Denton's reinterpret traditional Italian elegance and somehow manage to merge the soul of Milan with the spirit of New York.

Established NYC translated this into a corporate image: The use of gold and playful golden script above the bar and on some of the restaurant accessories is a nod to the opulence of Milan's glitterati scene; the overall typographic simplicity and straight lines of the simple rectangle logo reflect the toned down classiness of New York and the premium cuisine of the restaurant itself.

Honor

New York City, USA

RoAndCo, 2010 (ongoing)

Honor is a high-end women's luxury brand launched by designer Giovanna Randall in 2010. RoAndCo Studio assisted Giovanna in developing the brand from the very early stages and created a corporate identity that translates her vision into the graphic representation of the brand: Bridging gaps between exuberance and subtlety, tradition and freshness, sophistication and fun, Honor's corporate aesthetic combines the visual flair of the old-world atelier with a contemporary, authentic, and very personal feel.

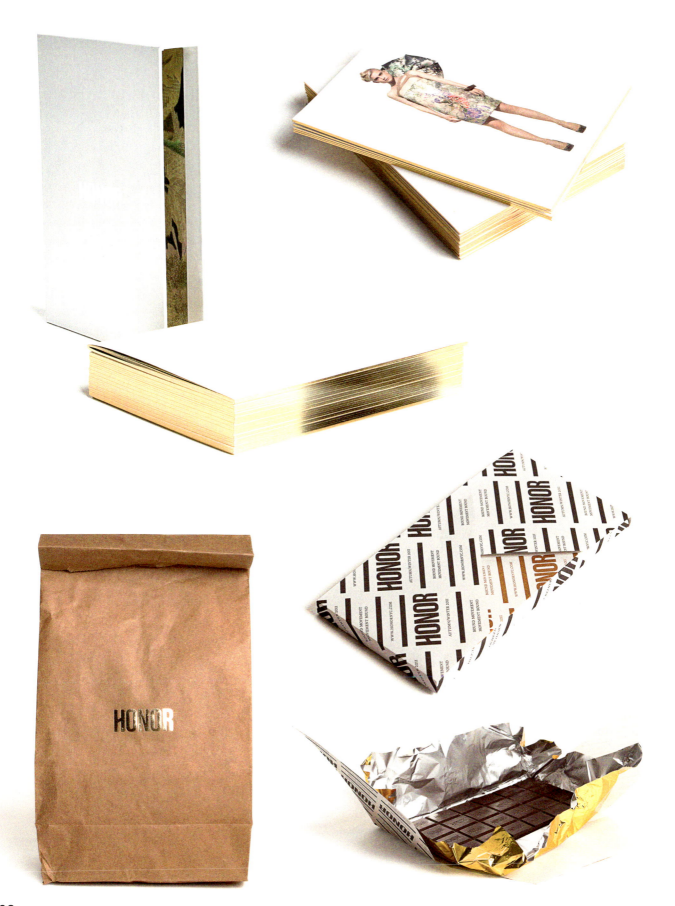

The Depart-
ment Store

Auckland, New Zealand

Brogen Averill, 2009

A collaboration of fashion designer Karen Walker, hair stylist Stephen Marr, and Dan Gosling of the successful Black Box boutique, the Department Store is their modern take on the traditional department store experience, their response to a world overwhelmed by generic product and bland shopping experiences. Brogen Averill's branding strategy underlines the approach by means of a simple unobtrusive aesthetic to define the stationery, the product labels and hangtags, the signage system of black-and-white light boxes, as well as the store's own newspaper.

Pedro
García

Barcelona, Spain

Clase BCN, 2005

Pedro García is a family business in its third generation. The first Pedro opened a children's shoes workshop in Elda, sister Mila and his partner Dale Dubovich. With an artistic direction geared towards the realm of high fashion, and an end product of impeccable quality, Pedro García's rebranding needed to combine the traditional core of the business with a new spirit of luxury. To meet this demand, Clase BCN developed a distinctive corporate language based on classic simplicity and under-

"Zapateros. That's pretty much how the folks at Pedro García define themselves. Shoemakers, in the most traditional sense of the term… and the most avant-garde sense of the term. At the helm now is the third generation of a family devoted to footwear."

Alicante, in 1925; the second Pedro took over the reins of his father's business in 1954 to specialize in women's footwear and introduce his collections to the international market; the third and latest Pedro so far manages the company together with his

stated elegance, a black-and-white palette, and the combination of different weights and variations of a time-tested serif typeface. A text block containing the full address and details of the company becomes the unpretentious yet classy logo.

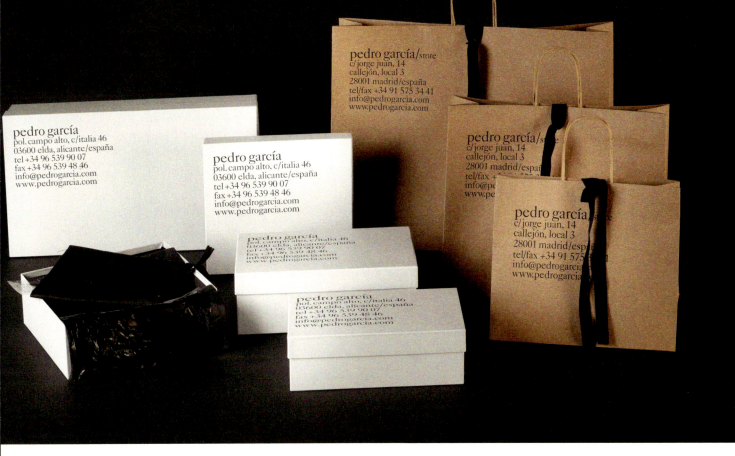

Anett Hajdu

Budapest, Hungary

Kissmiklos, 2011

Anett Hajdu sees her accessories as a juxtaposition to the visual chaos of contemporary eclectic fashion trends. Inspired by nature and the traditional dress of people closely in touch with it, especially those of Arctic tribes, she aims to give her collection a pleasant, pure aesthetic. Tuning in to this feel and taking it as a basis for his work, Kissmiklos developed Anett's branding strategy and designed the packaging concept for her 2011/12 Fall-Winter collection.

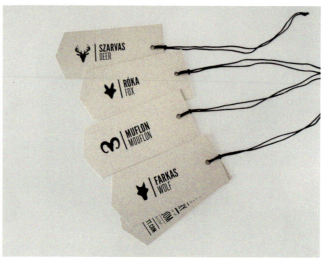

"In the chaos caused by contemporary and eclectic fashion trends, it is a pleasant feeling to turn toward the style of puritanism."

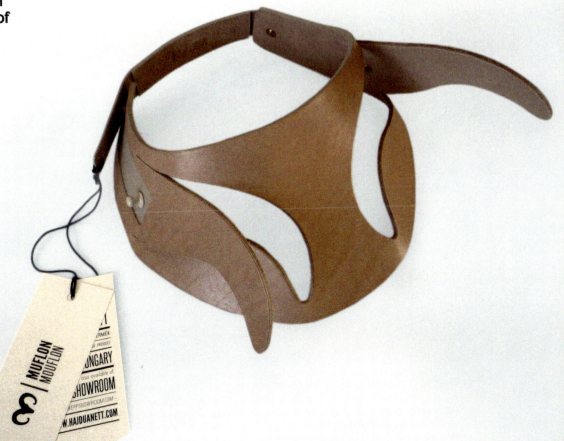

99

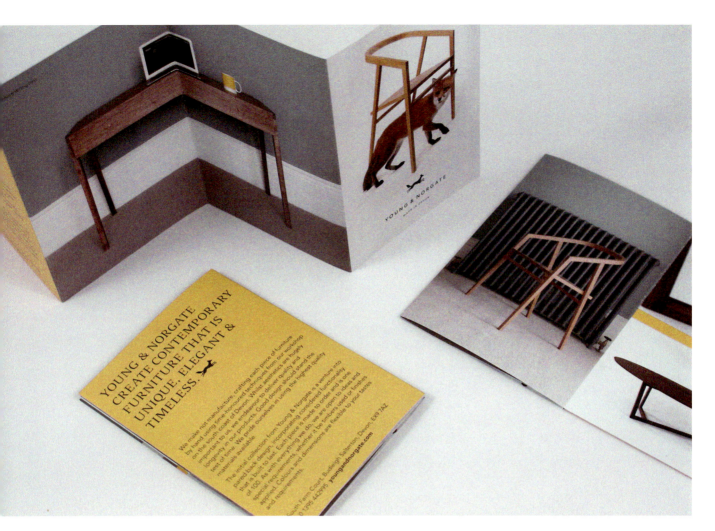

YOUNG & NORGATE

MADE IN DEVON

Young & Norgate

Devon, UK

A-Side Studio, 2011

Young & Norgate are a small group of designers and craftsmen. From their rural workshop on the south coast of Devon, they create contemporary furniture that is unique, elegant, and timeless, crafting each piece of furniture by hand using time-honored techniques. Aesthetics are hugely important to them, so they brought in A-Side Studio to develop a minimal but unique corporate image.

The pieces of Young & Norgate's collection have a delicate look and the attention to subtleties makes the ever alert and small-boned fox a worthy brand representative. As the protagonist of Young & Norgate's corporate image, it leaps forward to represent a company that is on the move. As a simplified logo mark the fox is used as distinct branding device on Young & Norgate's products.

The Haberdasher

Vancouver, Canada

Paone Creative, 2010

The Haberdasher is a men's fashion boutique offering traditional services. As an antiquated term for a dealer in men's clothing, the name Haberdasher suggests the traditional approach of the business. Along these lines, the visual identity by Paone Creative deliberately contradicts the slick design and impersonal feel of contemporary apparel chains and department stores. Instead, it responds to a resurgent trend towards traditional, wholesome values and a new sense of community. In terms of the company's core value of traditional, first-class service—friendly, personal, and tailored to particular client needs—the logo focuses on the client: Adapting the general stylistics of a traditional trademark, it shows a simple reverse silhouette of a man in a top hat, hidden within the unobtrusive appearance of a typographic monogram.

Someone wants you to look good... really good.

ABOUT YOUR WARBY PARKER GIFT CARD

1
Visit warbyparker.com and Shop
Find the perfect pair of glasses at www.warbyparker.com by using
our Virtual Try-On tool or signing up for our Home Try-On program

2
Using Your Gift Card
After selecting your glasses, simply enter the code on
the back of your gift card during the checkout process

3
Buy a Pair | Give a Pair
For every pair ordered, Warby Parker will donate
a pair of glasses to someone in need

Questions? Call us at (888) 492-7297

WARBY PARKER

Warby Parker

New York City, USA

The Bear Cave, 2010

Warby Parker is the collaborative project of four close friends who believe that everyone has the right to see. In response to the unfortunate fact that millions of people around the world today don't have access to proper vision care, they conceived an alternative to the overpriced eyewear of grabby market leaders. As if that weren't enough, for every pair of their vintage-inspired frames sold they donate a pair of glasses to someone in need through various non-profits. Warby Parker's first collection consists of 27 limited run styles and one monocle. The aesthetic is vintage-inspired with a fashion-forward twist.

The Bear Cave teamed up with the co-founders as the creative force to launch the brand off the ground. Keeping Warby Parker's core values in mind, they helped form the name,

brand identity, web design, art direction, lookbook, and campaign. The result is a sophisticated and unified vision.

Copenhagen Parts

Copenhagen, Denmark

Goodmorning Technology, 2009/2010

Copenhagen Parts produces innovative biking gear that combines urban mobility, functionality, and style. The bike enthusiasts who run the Copenhagen-based design studio Goodmorning Technology launched the small independent bicycle brand in 2009 and found themselves confronted with a tricky task: They wanted a robust, professional corporate image that would attract a broad range of customers, but by no means weaken their credibility as a supplier to the underground bicycle community. The result is a playful typographic interpretation of bike culture: Real bicycle connoisseurs are always on the lookout for special parts. Their bikes are subjects of an ongoing process of deconstruction and recombination and are never complete.

Alongside all visual communications, Goodmorning Technology designed the Bike Porter, a custom-made handlebar with integrated basket, to pilot Copenhagen Parts' product range.

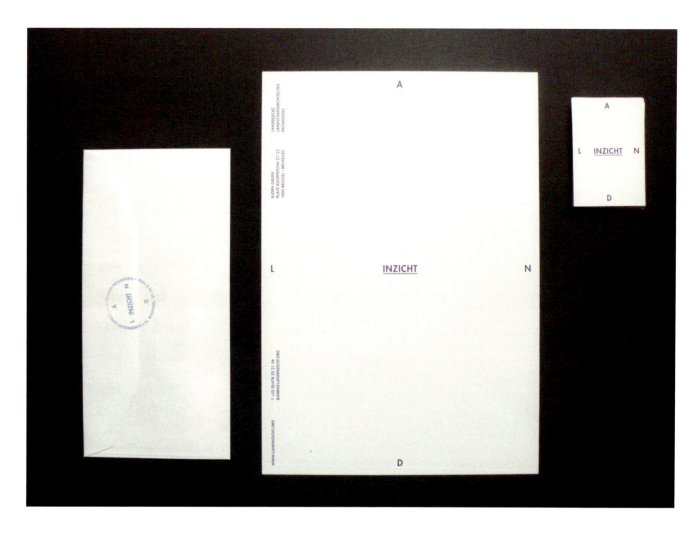

Landinzicht

Brussels, Belgium

**Manuela Dechamps Otamendi,
2010**

Landinzicht is a small landscape architecture firm founded in 2004 in Brussels. The name is based on the fusion of two Dutch words: *land,* meaning the same as it does in English, and *inzicht,* meaning knowledge or understanding. Defining the key aspects of Landinzicht's work, the two terms form the basis of the company's corporate identity. In designing it, Manuela Dechamps Otamendi paid particular attention to spatial relations and arrangement: The positioning of "inzicht" indicates the central significance of knowledge and understanding—in other words professionalism, a strong skill base, and sensitivity towards landscapes and nature—in Landinzicht's approach. The organization of the letters of "land" is inspired by compass points and thus serves as a visual reminder of a fundamental tool of the trade. Treated as a spatial concept rather than a composition of fixed elements, the brand mark is endlessly variable.

Spatial relations change with specific applications, typographic elements move away or towards each other according to the shape and size of their medium.

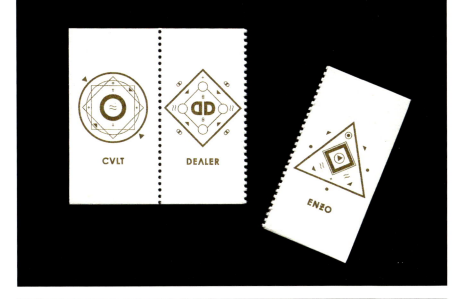

Cult Dealer Enzo

Utrecht, Netherlands

Drawswords, 2011

Cult Dealer Enzo is an event and workshop space located in a storage yard in the center of Utrecht. The name stands for the pillars of its threefold concept: Cult, an experimental lab for creative talent in Utrecht. Dealer, as a dealer of concepts, formats, and dreams. And Enzo, which is always a surprise for everyone involved. Asked to develop a brand identity for Cult Dealer Enzo, Drawswords created a series of icons: one for Cult, one for Dealer, one for Enzo. Adapting the stylistics of occult symbolism, these icons can be used individually or in any preferred combination.

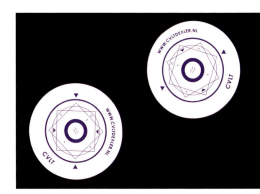

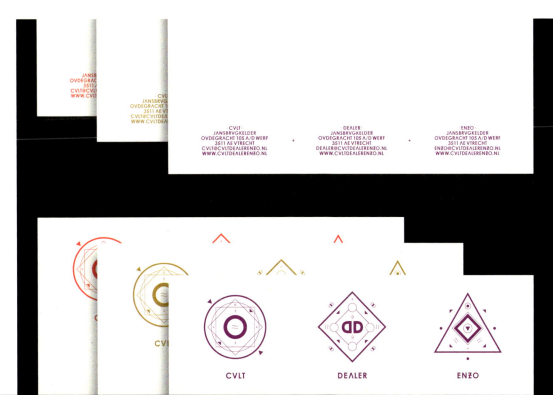

SOL

Wochenendtasche, mit robusten Griffen, vergrösserbar, mit Baumwoll-innenfutter, eine Aussentasche A4, eine Innentasche, alle mit Reissver-schluss, verstellbarer Schultertrag riemen. 44 cm x 45 cm x 20 cm

SOLITO

Sporttasche, mit robusten Griffen, vergrösserbar, mit Baumwoll-innenfutter, eine Aussentasche A4, eine Innentasche, alle mit Reissver-schluss, verstellbarer Schultertrag riemen. 44 cm x 45 cm x 20 cm

MOLL

Alltagstasche, gefüttert mit Ruck-sackstoff, mit Reissverschluss schliessbar, mit robusten Griffen, eine offene Aussentasche, eine Innentasche mit Reissverschluss, eine offene Innentasche. 40 cm x 31 cm x 10 cm

REMOLL

Alltagstasche, gefüttert mit Ruck-sackstoff, mit Reissverschluss schliessbar, mit robusten Griffen, eine offene Aussentasche, eine Innentasche mit Reissverschluss, eine offene Innentasche. 35cm x 30cm x 10 cm

AKT

Aktentasche, gefüttert mit Rucksackstoff, mit Reissverschluss schliessbar, mit robusten Griffen, verstellbarer Schulter-tragriemen, eine geschlossene Aussen-tasche A5, eine Innentasche mit Reissverschluss, eine offene Innentasche. 40 cm x 31 cm x 10 cm

LUNA

Damentasche, mit Baumwoll innenfutter, Innentasche, alle mit Reissverschluss, verstellbarer Schultertragriemen. 44 cm x 45 cm x 20 cm

REP

Wochenendtasche, mit robusten Griffen, vergrösserbar, mit Baumwoll-innenfutter, eine Aussentasche A4, eine Innentasche, alle mit Reissver-schluss, verstellbarer Schultertrag riemen. 44 cm x 45 cm x 20 cm

LONI

Wochenendtasche, mit robusten Griffen, vergrösserbar, mit Baumwoll-innenfutter, eine Aussentasche A4, eine Innentasche, alle mit Reissver-schluss, verstellbarer Schultertrag riemen. 44 cm x 45 cm x 20 cm

PFLEGE

Alle Taschen werden in kleinen Familienbetrieben in Zentralamerika, momentan Costa Rica, gefertigt. Die Erscheinung des Leders variiert stark. Ebenso ändert das Innenfutter je nach Verfügbarkeit und Hersteller. Auf irgendeine noch so kleine Art ist deshalb jede Tasche ein Einzelstück.

KONTAKT

Informationen und Bestellungen bei:
Anja Meyer &
Urs Hugentobler
CH - 8037 Zürich
Habsburgstrasse 1
+41 (0) 78 789 51 46
hello@bolsopaseo.com
www.bolsopaseo.com

Gestaltung: Esther Rieser, Zürich
Fotografie Cover: Sibylle Meier, Zürich
Innenseits, Judith Stadler, Zürich

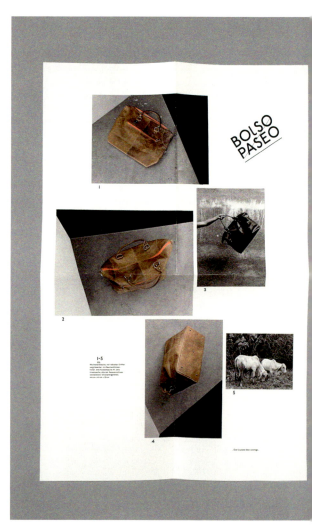

BOLSO
PASEO

1-5

BOLSO
PASEO

WWW.
BOLSO
PASEO.
COM

ZU
GAST
BEI

WWW.
BITS-
AND-
BOBS.
CH

BITS & BOBS

AN DER
ZURLINDENSTR. 230
8003 ZÜRICH

ÖFFNUNGSZEITEN
FR. 24.6 UM 11.30-18.30
SA. 25.6 UM 10.00-16.00

2011

Bolsopaseo

Zurich, Switzerland

Esther Rieser, 2009 (ongoing)

Bolsopaseo combines two Italian words: *bolso,* which means bag/pouch, and *paseo,* which means stroll/excursion. Visually connected by a diagonal line, the two expressions introduce the company's product: simple, sturdy bags that are, above all, practical and comfortable to wear.

Bolsopaseo's corporate identity was developed and executed by Esther Rieser.

Combining plain bold type and relatively fine line elements, the designer draws on the simplicity and sturdiness of her clients' products, and on the loving attention to detail that is key to Bolsopaseo's manufacturing process.

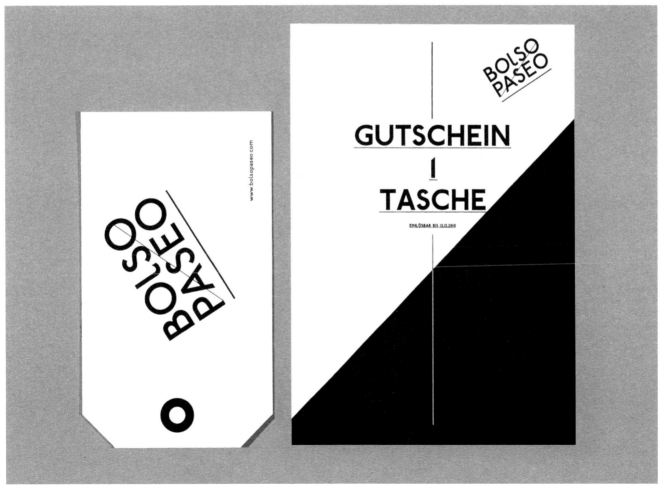

+
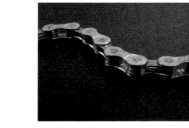
=

Ideafixed

Saint Petersburg, Russia

Orka, 2010

Many people are obsessed with bikes today, and so are the designers of the Orka Collective, who got to develop the branding strategy for the bike and repair shop of St. Petersburg's Fixed Gear community. Their concept picks up on the self-propelling dynamics of the bicycle culture and its flourishing entrepreneurialism. Drawing particularly on the way in which biking culture constantly reinvents itself, the logo takes inspiration from the Ouroboros, an ancient symbol depicting a serpent or dragon eating its own tail. The shop's self-reflective catchphrase "Everything is a cycle" takes the Ouroboros theme to extremes.

EVERYBODY IS DIFFERENT. BUT WE HAVE SOMETHING IN COMMON. WE NEED TO GET OUR SPEED FIX. IDEA FIXED IS A FIXED GEAR BIKE SHOP— WE OFFER ALL FIXIE PRODUCTS AND PARTS, COMPLETE BICYCLES AND OTHER STUFF. BUY FIXED GEAR EQUIPMENT ONLINE OR AT ONE OF OUR STORES. ALSO YOU CAN GET YOUR BIKE SERVICED IN OUR REPAIR SHOP AT ANY HOUR OF THE DAY.

IDEAFIXED
EST 2005

MAINTENAN...

FIXED GEAR | SINGLE SPEED

BASIC TUNE-UP	$20
MAJOR TUNE-UP	$40
COMPLETE OVERHAUL	$70
DRIVE TRAIN CLEANING	$25
WHEEL BUILD	$35
BIKE BUILD	$70

BRAKE REPL...
SPOKE REPLA...
TIRE SEALANT
TUBE | TIRE
FORK
BAR TAPE

BIKE CONVERSION
WHEEL TRUING
BRAKE | HUB ADJ.

ALL REPAIRS

47 STONELAND AVENUE
ST PETERSBURG 194100
936 78 64 · 936 55 78
IDEAFIXED INFO@GMAIL.COM
IDEAFIXED.COM

IDEAFIXED
EST 2005

IDEAFIXED
EVERYTHING IS A CYCLE

Senteurs d'Ailleurs

Brussels, Belgium

Codefrisko, 2011

Senteurs d'Ailleurs is an independent niche perfume and niche cosmetics store that opened its doors in 2011. A distinct corporate identity developed and implemented by Codefrisko presents the business as one of tradition and exclusiveness. Adapting the visual language of the occult, the logo combines a set of old-style illustrations in a diamond-shaped emblem. All illustrative elements can be swapped, switched, and moved around, which allows for an indefinite number of logo variations. Reproduced as stamps and stickers, they can also be individually applied on all kinds of media.

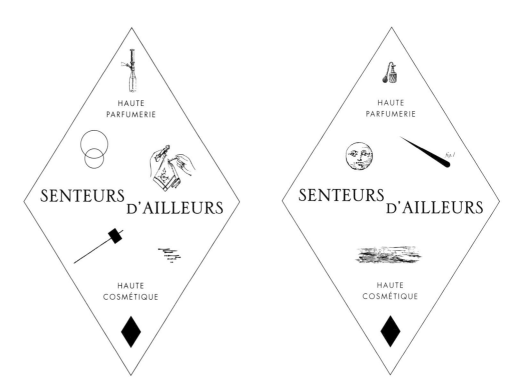

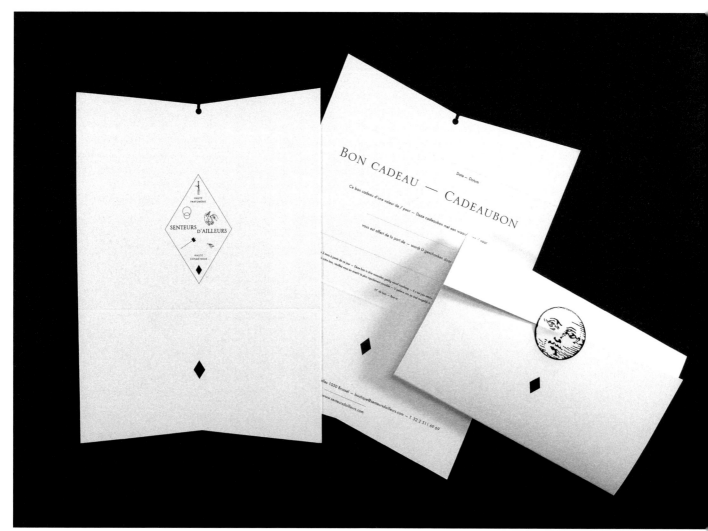

Alexandre Samuel

Brussels, Belgium

Codefrisko, 2010

Alexandre Samuel is a Brussels-based architect. To make his one-man business stand out from the wealth of competitors, he asked Codefrisko to equip him with a unique and striking corporate identity. The result includes a set of business cards, letterpressed onto two different types of paper and then glued together to give them an unusual and distinctive touch. Another highly individual element is the large logo stamp that enables Alexandre Samuel to conveniently print and reprint stationery and other branded material.

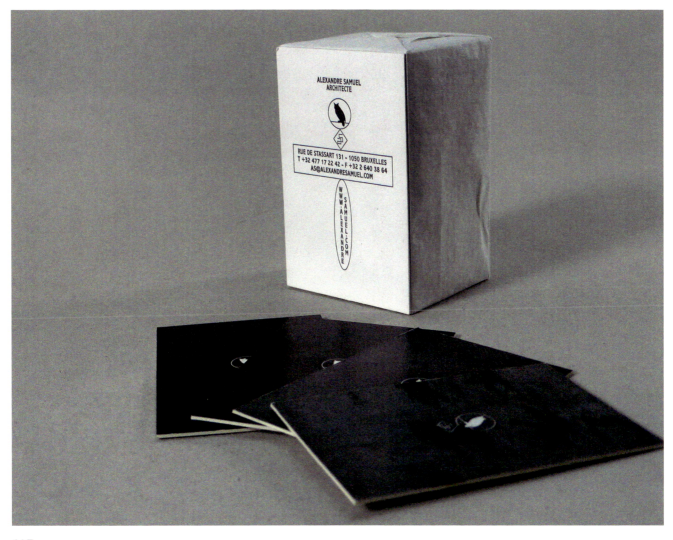

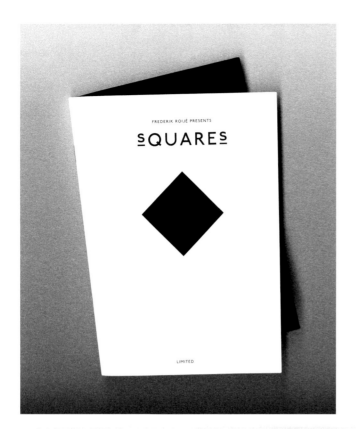

Frederik Roijé

Amsterdam, Netherlands

Lesley Moore, 2009

Frederik Roijé opened his studio in Amsterdam in 2003. Specialized in interiors, product design, and innovative concepts, the small studio has grown into an international design agency offering its services to both large companies and private clients. Besides the contract work, the company creates, sells, and distributes a varied collection of furniture, lighting, and accessories—all under the brand label Frederik Roijé.

Commissioned with its visual representation, Lesley Moore plays on the double meaning of the word "present": As a designer, Frederik Roijé presents work to an audience; as a maker of desirable products, he creates presents. Wrapping paper and a pop-up effect add an element of suspense to his business's corporate identity.

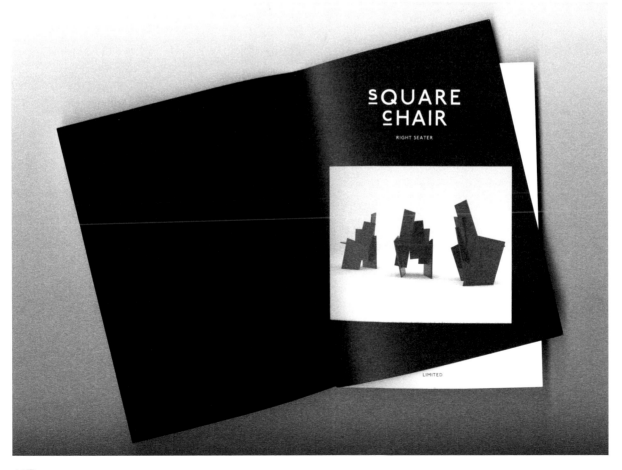

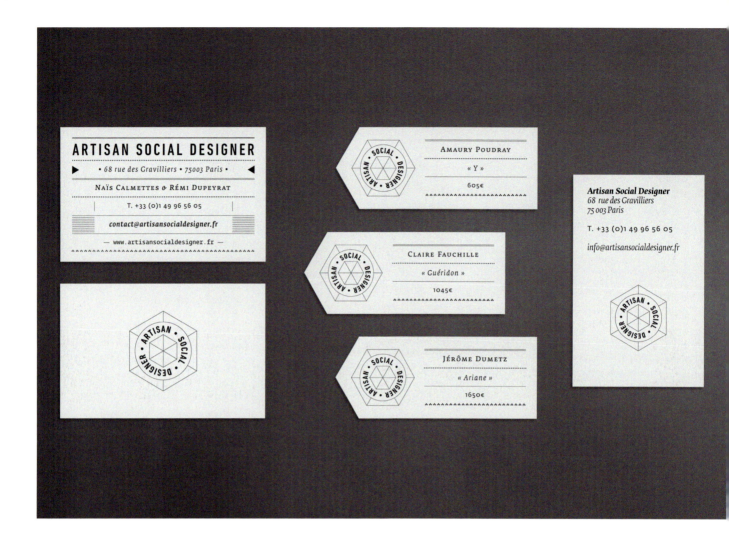

Artisan
Social
Designer

Paris, France

Nøne Futbol Club, 2011

Artisan Social Designer is a new concept store and gallery space in Paris. With the mission of promoting emerging forms of contemporary craft practices, this vibrant platform for creative talent sells and exhibits the work of young designers. The plain and straightforward brand identity by Nøne Futbol Club combines the language of traditional craft trade societies with that of contemporary visual arts—black and white, fresh and official, classic yet avant-garde.

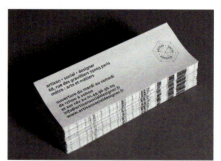

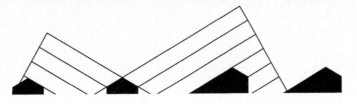

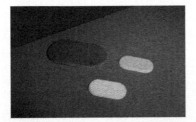  

ARTISAN SOCIAL DESIGNER

▶ est un tout nouveau concept-store ◀

CONSACRÉ UNIQUEMENT

| aux pratiques artisanales |

CONTEMPORAINES

— www.artisansocialdesigner.fr —

Ouverture le 17 Juin
12h00 — 22h00

Artisan Social Designer
68 rue des Gravilliers
75 003 Paris

T. +33 (0) 1 49 96 56 05

info@artisansocialdesigner.fr

polka gelato

polka

polka

polka

polka

Polka Gelato

London, UK

Vonsung, 2011

Polka Gelato offers "artisan," handcrafted ice cream for take away and home delivery, but the outstanding interior design of its Central London venue invites customers to eat in. Placing great value on what they call a "special gelato experience," the leading minds of the business commissioned Vonsung with the development of an extensive branding strategy.

Taking the client's notion of "artisan ice cream" as their starting point, the designers took inspiration from both artisan workshop spaces and the product itself: Raw concrete and rough walls are contrasted with the fluid shapes of custom furniture and the quirky line drawings on the printed material, elements that seem to resemble the sculpted nature of handmade gelato. The black-and-white palette used for the interior and graphics makes the colorful ice cream cabinet come to the fore, and with it the wide range of unconventional flavors.

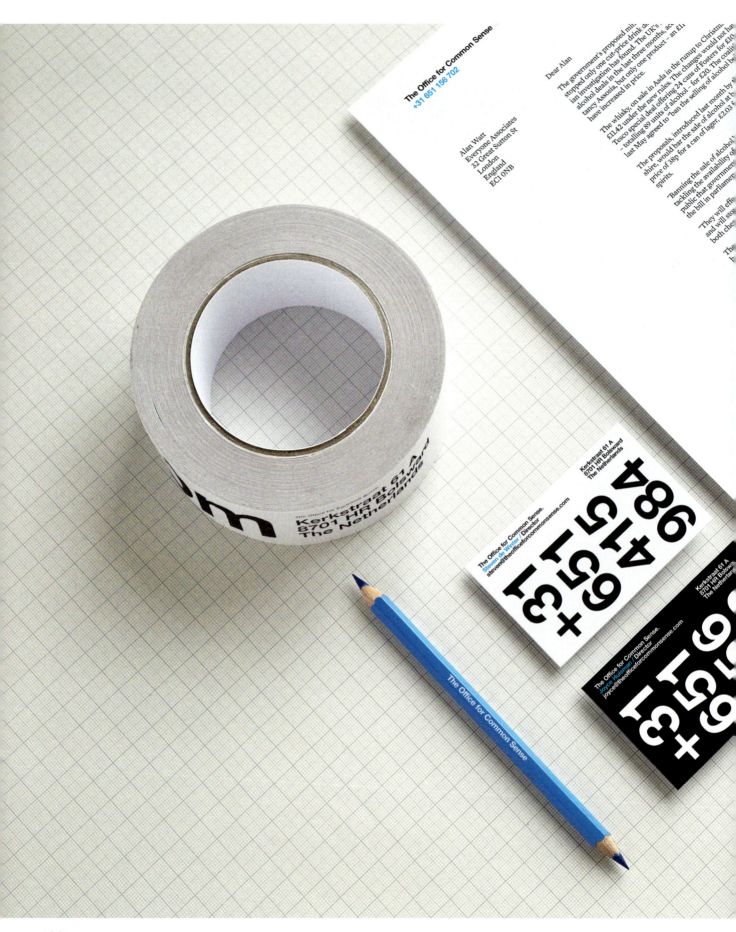

Kerkstraat 61 A
8701 HR Bolsward
The Netherlands

The Office
for Common
Sense

Bolsward, Netherlands

Everyone Associates, 2011

The Office for Common Sense is a creative business consultancy established and run by Dutch entrepeneur Joyce Huisman and her partner Steven. Everyone Associates approached the office's branding strategy full of ideas, metaphors and potential logos that would represent the concept of common sense. Taking a step back, they reached the conclusion that a pragmatic, straightforward derivation would suit the subject matter much better than a definite brand mark. So they asked themselves some fundamental questions: What is the most important piece of information on a business card after the name? The phone number. What is the most straightforward, common sense font? Helvetica. And what is the most straightforward, common sense way to represent the collaboration of the office's two partners? A double-sided business card with Joyce's details on one side, Steven's on the other.

When Joyce runs out of cards she just steals some of Steven's rather than print more. Common sense. Likewise, if one end of the office's branded pencils gets blunt you can still use the other end. Common sense.

Micheline

San Pedro Garza García, Mexico

Anagrama, 2010

Micheline is a print shop dedicated to designing and printing stationery and related products for social events. Opening up to a younger target group, the team behind Micheline asked Anagrama to refresh their corporate image. The graphically sophisticated, eclectic result speaks to potential customers of all generations.

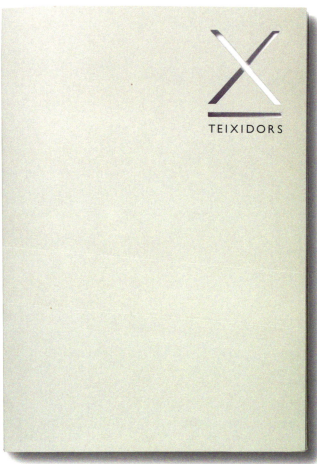

Teixidors

Barcelona, Spain

Clase BCN, 2008

Teixidors' unique fabrics are the result of an entirely manual process and highest quality materials. Inspired by the refined simplicity of their products, Clase BCN chose clear forms and a very clean and fine typeface for the key elements of Teixidors brand identity.

Borrowing the most notable letter of the company's name, the x shape of the logo refers to the basic component of weaving, which is the fundamental work process of Teixidors. The image photography uses natural light, cleanliness, and cool simplicity to contrast the range of hand-woven blankets, pillows, and curtains.

Alfonso López y Asociados S.L.

Barcelona, Spain

Folch Studio, 2010

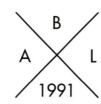

BUFETE ALFONSO LÓPEZ

Since its formation in 1991, the office of Alfonso López y Asociados S.L. has been providing legal advice and financial consulting services to small and mid-sized companies. The philosophy of the office is based on the Catholic Church's social doctrine, following the principles of honesty, professional integrity, and social justice. The corporate identity by Folch studio is minimal and elegant. Whether the x shape of the logo is in fact a tilted cross to reference Alfonso López's Christian mindset is an open question.

128

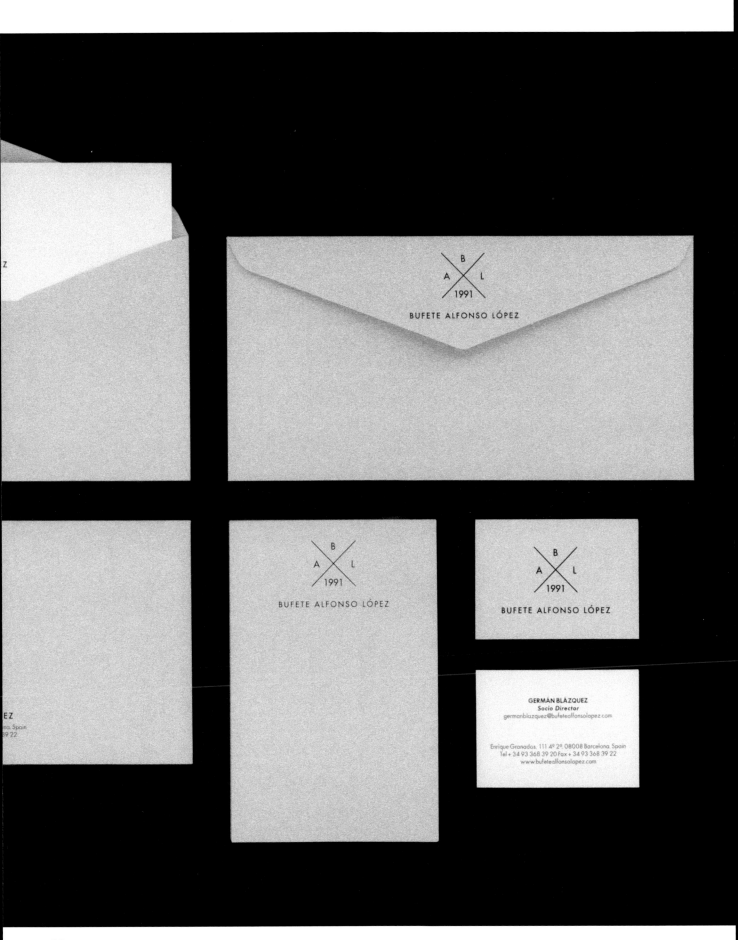

Sense of Beauty

Graz, Austria

Moodley Brand Identity, 2009

"Beauty without a scalpel" is the motto of the new beauty parlor Sense of Beauty in Graz. The owner, Dr. Przemyslaw Strulak and his team are known for natural and gentle beauty and cosmetic treatments and their rejection of hard technology and expensive products.

For their corporate image, Moodley Brand Identity developed an aesthetic that portrays the theme of beauty in a subtle, sensitive, and emotional way. The clean black logo mark is contrasted with a natural skin background color to combine professionalism and sensuousness.

L'É LOI

L'Éloi

Montreal, Canada

Feed, 2010

Founded in 2001 as an artist representation service combined with a production company, L'Éloi has grown into a renowned agency representing some of the best Canadian photography artists and stylists. The mission is to "guide artists so they can achieve their full potential and make their dream come true." This notion of subtle guidance is fundamental to the corporate image Feed created for the agency: The visual precedence of the logo reflects the personality of the client; the clean, minimalist overall aesthetic leaves room for the photographs to speak for themselves.

Michael Sontag

Berlin, Germany

Eps51 Graphic Design Studio,
2011

The fashion designer Michael Sontag thinks of his work as a fluent process detached from parameters such as seasons, trends, and target groups. This approach is reflected in an assertive, straight visual language—both regarding his collection and his corporate image.

Eps51 designed a signet and logotype portraying Michael Sontag's initials in custom glyphs to be used in diverse combinations on different types of media. Christian Schwarzenberg's atmospheric photography completes the brand identity.

MY FITNESS

And Larry, 2010

MY Fitness is a holistic dance and fitness studio for all ages. Based on the initials of its founder and managing director May Yang, MY is a very personal mark. And Larry's visual identity translates May Yang's approach to her dance and fitness instruction: clarity and simplicity are key.

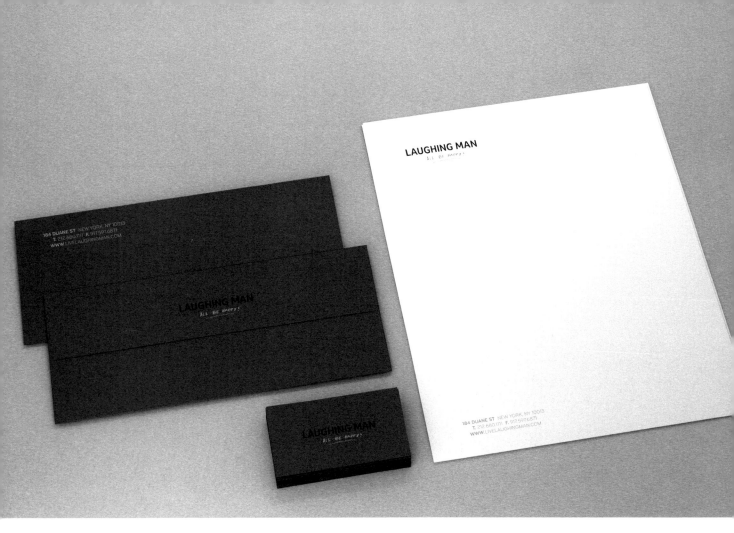

Laughing Man

New York City, USA

Established NYC, 2011

Laughing Man Coffee and Tea is the first company of Laughing Man, a charity project founded and run by film and theater star Hugh Jackman. Featuring a wide array of fair trade products from farms in Ethiopia, Peru, Guatemala, Papua New Guinea and beyond, Laughing Man has

the motto "All be happy."

Established NYC developed a brand identity along the lines of Laughing Man's mission. The collection of packaging is both joyful and friendly. Custom chalk type elements connote the idea of a hand-finished barista quality. Casually applied and constantly

changing laughing face stickers on each product reflect the company's ethical-mindedness and invite the consumer to interact with the brand directly by uploading their own laughing face on the website for a chance to be used on future packaging.

HOME BLEND

SMILE !   HOME BLEND

LAUGH !   EXPRESSO

ALL BE HAPPY !   EXPRESSO

                           DECAF !

                           DECAF !

LAUGHING
MARKETPLAC

COFFEE
CAPPUCINO
LATTE
MOCHA
HOT CHOC
STEAM MILK
AMERICANO
ESPRESSO
DBL ESPR
MACHIATO
TEA
CHAI LATTE

Maria
Vogel

Monterrey, Mexico

Anagrama, 2010

Maria Vogel is an up-and-
coming Latin American fashion designer. Her designs are
imposing, and she needed a
convincing brand image to accompany the collection without
competing with it. Anagrama's
solution is subtle and sober,
while still remaining in tune with
Maria's avant-garde vision.

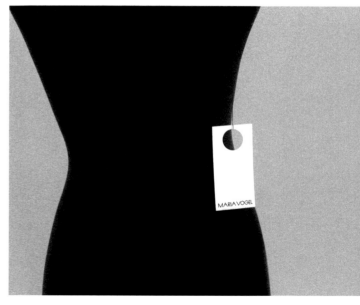

Aker Brygge

Oslo, Norway

Bleed, 2011

Aker Brygge is not a business but a city district of Oslo. To promote the distinctive area as a distinctive brand, the designers of studio Bleed focused on what had previously been defined as Aker Brygge's core values: its history, its craftmanship, and its contrasts. The result is a considerable range of corporate tools including stationery, a publication, a line of branded promotional products, and a custom font.

HISTORY/ CRAFTMANSHIP/ CONTRAST/

Deli
Rant

Valencia, Spain

Estudio M Llongo, 2010

The restaurant and delicatessen shop is housed in a former commercial space, tucked away down a side street in the historic heart of Valencia. The first visual impression is of an industrial aesthetic: brick walls, marble floors, and construction elements. Contrasting the bleak, cool interior of the restaurant with illustrations in the style of Dada and motley vintage furniture, Estudio M Llongo succeeded in creating an individual and highly emotive branding solution. It invites guests to sit, eat, and dreamily stare at what appears to be a whale sandwich (in which the whale is swimming happily upside down). Or at one of the other visuals scattered across the walls of the venue.

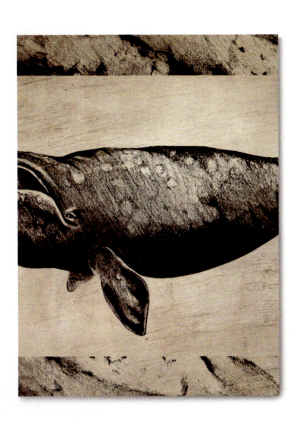

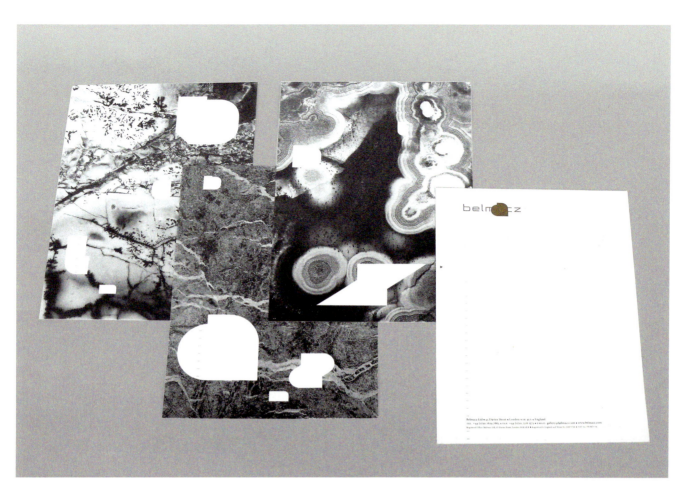

New logo concept

Shop card

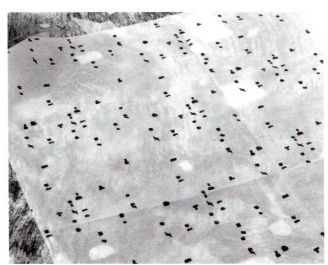

Wrapping paper detail

Belmacz

London, UK

Mind Design, 2011

Julia Muggenburg is the creative force behind Belmacz, a London-based jewelry company that opened its first shop and gallery in Mayfair in 2011. As well as jewelry, Belmacz offers a range of beauty preparations—balms, creams, and glosses enriched with gold, crushed pearls, and powdered gemstones. Julia considers Belmacz a creative agenda—a cult, in which she harnesses alchemic powers of creativity and craft to transform both base and precious materials into objects of beauty and desire.

Just like Julia, Mind Design focuses on Belmacz's cult, rather than on its presentation as a luxury brand. Retaining the original logo, Mind Design added a variety of coarse letter shapes that refer to the process in which raw minerals and diamonds are refined until they become a piece of jewelry. Inspired by the shape of mines and the act of mining where massive holes are brutally "cut out" of the earth, they introduced harsh contrasts and glaring, hole-like shapes to Belmacz's brand identity. As a conceptual gimmick, all cutouts are kept to reappear across the different items and media of visual communication. For example, a missing bit on a business card becomes part of the design of a carrier bag.

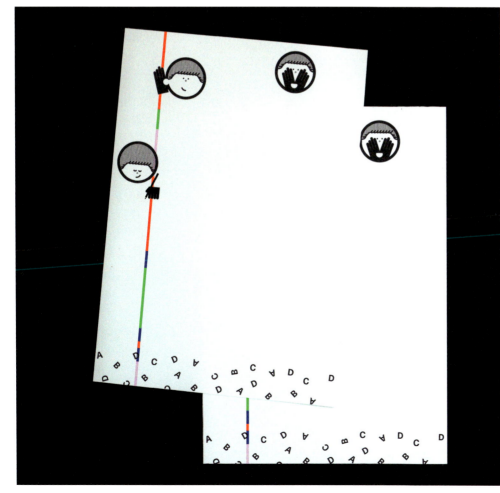

The Playlist Generation

New York City, USA

RoAndCo, 2009

The Playlist Generation is a sonic branding company founded by DJ Michael Smith. Together with a team of other experienced DJs, music supervisors, producers, remixers, recording engineers, composers, music publishers, music critics, and bloggers, Smith specializes in developing and executing event soundtracks and sonic identities for companies as diverse as ABC Network, Louis Vuitton, and The Standard Hotel Group.

While a large part of the music business laments the distribution of music over the internet, The Playlist Generation's corporate identity by RoAndCo Studio takes the new way we consume music as a starting point. Clearly influenced by the aesthetics of the ipod era, a system of icons represents the music business and its ongoing technological developments, factoring in traditional instruments like drum circles as well as today's most common form of music distribution, the playlist.

ABCD

Lyon, France

FizzzBzzzz, 2007

ABCD supports children in the acquisition and development of language. FizzzBzzzz created a corporate identity for the association that represents the subject matter in a playful, straightforward manner: Human language is represented by the three capital letters ABC, a D is added to complete the brand's name. Randomly scattered over business cards and stationery, the letters hint at the complexity and infinite possible combinations of our language system. Iconographic illustrations of three children in action typify ABCD's young clientele.

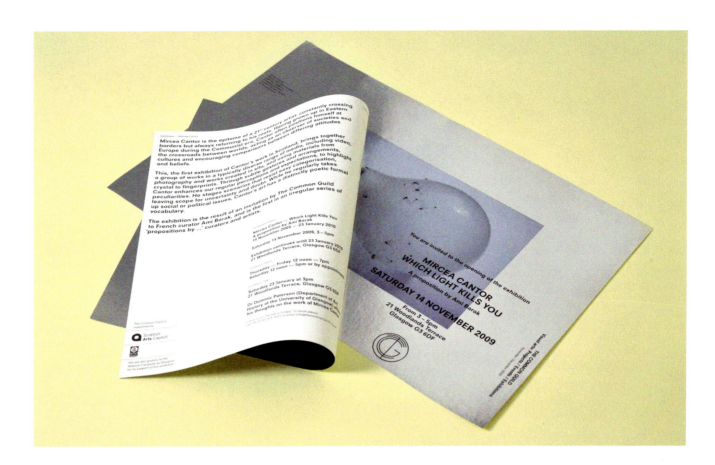

The Common Guild

Glasgow, Scotland

Marque, 2008 (ongoing)

The Common Guild is a visual arts organization established in 2006 in Glasgow. Presenting a dynamic, international program of contemporary visual art projects, exhibitions, and events, the organization felt the need to present itself with an appropriately sophisticated branding.

In reference to the name The Common Guild and the corresponding notion of an institutional association of craftsmen, Marque created a brand logo in the style of an official signet. The delicate line work can be stamped, etched, or embossed, and is used alongside a palette of three carefully chosen typefaces that allow for flexibility across different elements of the identity.

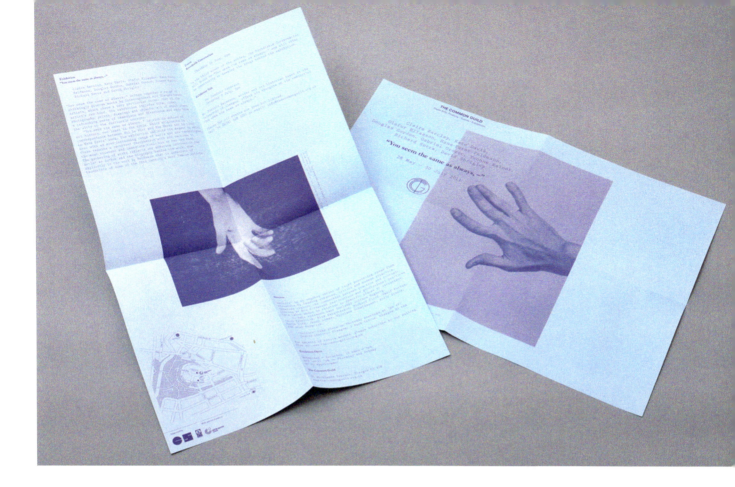

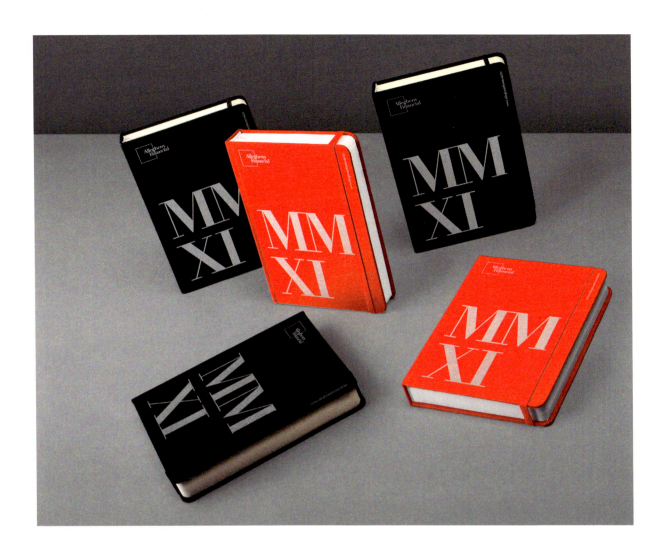

Allegheny Financial

Zagreb, Croatia

Bunch, 2011

Since it was launched in 1997, Allegheny Financial has offered an all-in-one service including market analysis, legal and tax advisory services, strategic investment, and project management for the real estate market. Having achieved a notably high market position, they asked Bunch to boost the company's status with a smart corporate identity solution. The visual strategy is based on contrasts: Harmonious and slightly understated overall stylistics are contrasted with vivid colors and glossy foil finishing, suggesting a combination of seriousness and briskness. The combination of bold and fine strokes of the classic typeface expresses solidity and reliability, as well as precision and loving attention to detail.

Ultimately, the concept of contrast itself creates a visual dynamic that reflects movement and growth as core competences of financial services and property development.

Ever‐
last‐
ing

Stählemühle, pp. 152–153

Cosmetics look like Nivea, coffee-to-go joints like Starbucks, hairdressers like Tony & Guy, and web designer's portfolios make use of gradients and glossy 3D buttons. The era of entrepreneurship is affected by general merchandise. Faceless, profit-hungry business conglomerates dominate the market and establish corporate trends that unify the appearance of individual business sectors. Many small businesses try to climb on the bandwagon, at least visually, adapting the sleek and seemingly impeccable aesthetics of high-price marketing strategies.

Others are proud to be different. Nonconformity becomes a core value, as do unevenness and imperfection. The result is a variety of brands that share a homespun appearance while taking very different directions. Jon Contino, for example, celebrates raw DIY aesthetics. His branding for the photographer Sven Hoffmann ✦ p. 162 uses handwritten type and a custom rubber stamp of genuine simplicity, his own brand CXXVI Clothing Co ✦ p. 163 solely consists of hand-made elements inspired by vintage American apparel and takes cues from traditional manufacturing processes of the clothing industry. The industrial workspace is an often-cited setting, one that also inspired Dan Blackman when developing the branding strategy for Hammarhead Motorcycles ✦ p. 170 or Glasfurd & Walker in setting the tone for Meat & Bread's ✦ p. 172 interior design. Le Tigre's branding for the Mariposa ✦ p. 188 pasta shop has a certain DIY charm, too, but focuses on the homely, organic feel of lovingly crafted elements. The rustic look of A Cowboy's Dream Bed and Breakfast, ✦ p. 154 as designed by Kuro, and the back-to-basics identity developed by Orka for the insurance company Vincent Trust ✦ p. 168 are grounded in old-time nostalgia.

Some small businesses featured in this section appear old-fashioned and slightly weathered, others rough and unpolished. Of course, in many cases, small brands are simply not able to pay for high-tech production processes, the newest materials, and expensive design studios to develop an ostentatiously luxurious brand performance and it would certainly be naive to ignore money as a defining force in this context. It is important to note, though, that rustic features are no means inevitably the result of office austerity measures, or an inveterate fear of progress. They are often, in fact, elements of deliberate design decisions that demonstrate how intriguing branding strategies do not have to depend on large budgets or fancy concepts. Restrictions can shape up as a benefit. The authentic, raw, and often romantic spirit of rustic elements can form an essential part of the brand identity. Sometimes, it is about staying true to the brand's heritage and its proven values. Sometimes, it is a matter of rejecting the frostiness of modern technology, its slick and unstained shapes and surfaces. More often than not, it turns out to be a well-considered brand strategy to win over the customer, who is fed up with perfect-looking whims and fancies, too.

"Created as a distinct departure from the typical salon, we ask our customers to sit back, relax, and enjoy a glass of wine."

New Vintage Beauty Lounge

Portland, USA

Chandelarrow, 2010

New Vintage Beauty Lounge is a high-end full service beauty salon and cosmetic boutique located in Northeast Portland. Founded by the newly-wed couple as a distinct departure from the conventional salon environment, and designed to appeal to both women and men, the Beauty Lounge brings together a range of different styles: Vintage thrift store furniture is combined with mid-century modern pieces and symbols borrowed from the natural environment of the Pacific Northwest. The graphic identity by Chandelarrow focuses on tradition (vintage type), nature (antlers and dear head illustrations), and luxury (gold-and-black and sovereign emblems).

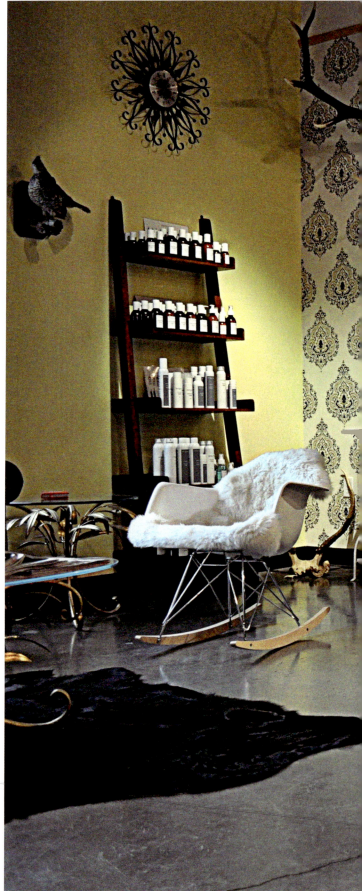

Stählemühle

MÜNCHHÖF IM HEGAU

AQUA VITAE

DESTILLAT N°:

112

Stählemühle

Mährische Vogelbeere aus dem Maulbeerfass

(Sorbus aucuparia var. moravica)

☒ BRAND ☐ GEIST ☐ MAZERIERT & DESTILLIERT ☐ MIT FRUCHTAUSZUG

☒ UNFILTRIERT ☐ LIKÖR ☐ FASSGELAGERT IN *Maulbeere*

ERNTEJAHR	FLASCHE N°:	DESTILLATEUR
2009	*38*	*ChKeller*

50 CL   42 % VOL.

CHRISTOPH KELLER & CHRISTIANE SCHOELLER · STÄHLEMÜHLE
78253 EIGELTINGEN-MÜNCHHÖF · WWW.STAEHLEMUEHLE.DE

Stählemühle

Eigeltingen, Germany

Christoph Keller, 2010

Christoph Keller switched from art publishing to operating an organic and sustainable distillery for finest fruit brandies, eau-de-vie, and world class spirits.

Having sold his own publishing house in Frankfurt, he moved with his family into a farm-like property on Lake Constance, that houses the distillery, tasting house, mills, and office building.

With only a small amount of land, the work of four hands (Keller's and his wife's), and a good deal of know-how, the Edelobstbrennerei Stählemühle has made its mark as one of the world's top distilleries.

Keller's branding for the Edelobstbrennerei Stählemühle combines simplicity with tradition. Since the distillery produces and distributes 80 different brandies in small, high quality batches, it was impossible to develop a unique label for each kind. Keller developed a label in style of a printed form, with blank spaces for filling in all the relevant specifications by hand. The bottles are inspired by old-time pharmacy vessels and include their practical features such as UV protection and the ability to pour small amounts. Small type on the cork of the bottles heralds the company's maxim "Ex Pluribus Unum"—out of many, one.

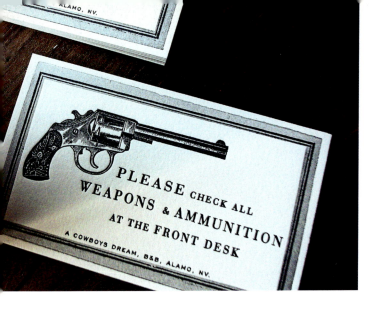

A Cowboy's Dream
Alamo, USA

Kuro, 2010

Phyllis Frias set out to create a memorial to her husband, the late Mr. Charlie Frias. The result is A Cowboy's Dream, a bed and breakfast venue located in the small town of Alamo, 90 miles north of Las Vegas.

The rustic, traditional amenities offer a Great Room, a charming Bunk House, a dance hall, and a wedding pavilion for special events. Hearty, decadent fare is served up in the old-time homey dining room. A smorgasbord of rustic found items is scattered all over the place.

Kuro created an identity of nostalgia that invites guests to become part of the Frias family's history and legacy. Every stay is a new narrative.

155

Michalovic Wood Art

Austin, USA

Arts & Recreation, 2010

"I started looking at woodworking as an artist and realized it was something I could do for a long time."

Aaron Michalovic is a trained timber framer whose clients range from individuals to commercial businesses. In keeping with the meticulous artistry of his labor, Michalovic calls his company Michalovic Wood Arts rather than Wood Works. Favoring antique hand tools to modern machinery, he approached Arts and Recreation to develop a brand identity that is in line with the values of traditional craftsmanship without compromising on a sophisticated and contemporary feel.

Mad
Brew

Cape Town, South Africa

Adam Hill, 2010

Mad Brew Productions started out as a live music events company and then also branched into other offerings: media, consisting of photography and music videos, as well as interiors. Adam Hill's rebranding is inspired by the concept of "wearing many hats." Taking up the aesthetic of a travelling Victorian salesman, the new visual identity neatly packages Mad Brew's different fields of business activity. A selection of vintage typefaces and a slightly weathered feel echo posters and sign writing of the bygone era to convey the idea of old-time showmanship.

The Hummingbird

Leeds, UK

Analogue, 2011

There is a three level restaurant and bar located in a small village two miles away from Leeds. The team behind it has a bit of history. Fifteen years ago they opened Oporto—young, vibrant, and a little rough around the edges. Next was Jake's Bar & Grill, then the Neon Cactus. Having developed a considerable sense of the market and a passion for fresh regional food, they now invite friends old and new to the Hummingbird.

Inspired by the restaurant's locally sourced food, its fine selection of mostly British beers, wines, and cocktails and its relaxed inviting atmosphere, Analogue designed a brand that expresses homeliness and tradition.

Betty & June

Abilene, USA

Ryan Feerer, 2011

Betty & June is a women's clothing boutique located in downtown Abilene, Texas. Its name is a homage to the owners' grandparents, its corporate identity thoughtfully considered and handcrafted by Ryan Feerer. As the store aims to give the customer a both personable and personal shopping experience, Ryan decided to have everything handmade: Although it meant a lot more work, all of the tags, bags, and business cards have been hand-stamped, the signage behind the cash wrap is hand-painted, telling Betty & June's story and personal anecdotes from the owners' grandparents lives. The scripty, feminine style of the typography is contrasted with an overall rustic feel.

PRESENTLY:..
....

O   Mobile telephone: (919) 360-9964
□   E-mail: **bob.massengale@gmail.com**
△   Post:..
/

PRESENTLY:..
....

O   Mobile telephone: (919) 360-9964
□   E-mail: **bob.massengale@gmail.com**
△   Post:..
/

PRESENTLY:..
....

O   Mobile telephone: (919) 360-9964
□   E-mail: **bob.massengale@gmail.com**
△   Post:..
/

PRESENTLY:..
....

O   Mobile telephone: (919) 360-9964
□   E-mail: **bob.massengale@gmail.com**
△   Post:..
/

PRESENTLY:............   PRESENTLY:............

Robert Massengale

Raleigh, USA

Joshua Gajownik, 2009

Robert Massengale lives and works as a polymath outdoorsman. To visually represent himself and his universal business as a brand, Massengale approached Joshua Gajownik. Focusing on the outdoorsman's myriad of abilities and his motto of "Anything, anyway," the designer developed a set of simple geometric permutations. As adaptable as the entrepreneur himself, this system enables Robert Massengale to make a business card out of anything that can be stamped: A recycled envelope, loose napkin, or the back of a receipt. The choice of material and a blank space for specifications on the back of the card invite the outdoorsman to adapt his identity to every job

and adventure. As many of his travels take Massengale to remote areas, he can mark the contact details on his cards as "active" or "not available."

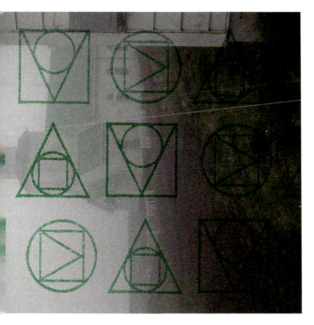

Sven Hoffmann

Hamburg, Germany

Jon Contino, 2010

The photographer Sven Hoffmann is an analogue, understated type of guy. To communicate himself and his studio to existing and potential clients, he envisioned something simple and rugged. And commissioning Jon Contino, he got it: A hand-drawn, typographic logo as the key visual, its minimal application on the front window of his studio as the basic signage, custom wooden logo stamps, and a set of large, unobtrusively branded matte postcards featuring Hoffmann's simple black-and-white photographs for basic promotion purposes.

CXXVI
Clothing Co.

New York City, USA

Jon Contino, 2011

New York-based line CXXVI produces American-made apparel with a matching aesthetic.

Co-founders Jon Contino and Matt Gorton ran the design studio Onetwentysix before they moved on to put together a convincing collection of vintage wash tee's, soft flannels, combed hoodies, and a considerable number of one-of-a-kind accessories. Everything from the products to the extensive set of collateral materials is completely hands-on and made in a small workshop: hand-stamped, hand-dyed, hand-sewn, etc. The overall aesthetic

is primarily inspired by CXXVI's traditional organic production processes and the brand's American heritage. Jon Contino developed a branding strategy that focuses on uniqueness, rather than fixed elements: Each product utilizes a different, specific take on the name and identity of the brand; the logo changes, while the overall style is kept similar enough to act as an identity unto itself. The specialization helps to separate and distinguish the various types of products the brand offers.

Custom wooden stamps are used as traditional hands-on branding devices and to support the value of CXXVI's handmade single pieces.

Schiller's Liquor Bar

New York City, USA

Mucca Design, 2003

Schiller's Liquor Bar is a casual neighborhood restaurant established and owned by Keith McNally. McNally and his two chefs Riad Nasr and Lee Hanson offer continental specialties for breakfast, brunch, lunch, dinner, and late night supper, as well as a seasonal list of house cocktails and three different wines—"cheap," "decent," and "good." "Cheap" is the best.

With a logo script reminiscent of a signature and a neon script version of it on the venue's façade, Schiller's feels like a family-owned downtown joint of a long bygone era. Other aspects of the restaurant's visual identity by Mucca Design relate to this sense of retro quirkiness. For example, the custom typeface with oddly sized and unevenly spaced letters that gives the menu a unique vintage look.

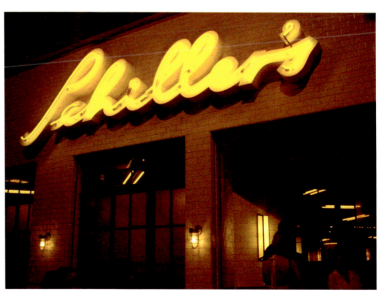

"Every aspect of the project was designed with a sense of home-made quirkiness."

Re-Cycles

Melbourne, Australia

Michael Longton, 2010

Re-Cycles is a Melbourne-based bicycle workshop founded and run by Mitch Farina. When it came to branding his business, Mitch approached his close friend Michael Longton, who created a corporate image that emphasizes the company's work process: Re-Cycles restores, repairs, and builds vintage bicycles, using traditional and hands-on techniques. To visualize this approach, Longton created an overall vintage aesthetic inspired by old auto workshops.

The
Abbott

Parkdale, Canada

Clean, 2011

The Abbott is a coffee shop in Parkdale, a suburb of Toronto. Its name pays homage to the first Afro-Canadian doctor, Anderson Ruffin Abbott. Besides being a doctor, Abbott wrote poetry and served in public office as well as in the Union Army to fight against slavery in the emerging United States of America. He was a Parkdale local, so his name attracts not only inquisitive tourists but also people from the neighborhood. Commissioned with creating The Abbott's corporate aesthetic, Clean defined Anderson Ruffin Abbott as the key element and developed a variety of icons, symbols, and phrases that represent the man and his time.

Vincent Trust

Saint Petersburg, Russia

Orka, 2010

Vincent Trust is an insurance company that specializes in life insurance, property management, and financial services. Inspired by the image of old, faithful Mr. Trust, who loves his local business and face-to-face contact with his clients, the corporate identity by Orka makes use of solid retro type, time-honored symbols of safety (rope and knot), and traditional means of—mainly regional—promotion, such as the newspaper classified.

Hammarhead Industries

Philadelphia, USA

Daniel Blackman, 2011

Hammarhead Industries build custom motorcycles that are simple yet modern and inspired by the iconic bikes of the 1950s. James Loughead founded the company with an eye towards repurposing, recycling, efficiency, and the mission of working beyond the "plastic-encrusted mainstream motorcycle industry." To reflect this mission visually, Dan Blackman refreshed Hammarhead's brand identity in a way that avoids the motorcycle industry's usual promotion clichés. A bold and basic logo mark goes along with a series of iconographic symbols and letterings to be used for in-store and workshop visuals, and as emblems on the staff's apparel, on product labels, and of course on the bikes.

"Most of our bikes are quiet, some are silent, and all are built to be ridden."

Meat & Bread

Vancouver, Canada

Glasfurd & Walker, 2010

Meat & Bread's owners Frankie Harrington and Cord Jarvie certainly have a back-to-basic approach to food. Since the venue opened in late 2010, their stripped-down menu offers a succinct but high-quality

selection of local free-range meat, served in a classy yet industrial ambience.

Glasfurd & Walker, commissioned by Harrington and Jarvie

"Meat & Bread is a simple and classic ode to the butcher shop."

to communicate the restaurant's raw and uncomplicated offer, took "strength through simplicity"

as their ultimate design mandate. Framing the general stylistics of the restaurant's signage and interior, products and packaging, stickers and stationery, this motto runs through the corporate identity as its central thread. With a focus on Meat & Bread's daily roasted meat, Glasfurd & Walker created a visual system to communicate changing offerings, and a series of icons to complement the core logo on menus and packaging for products and take out.

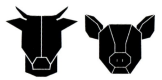

173

Tapas, 24

Barcelona, Spain

<u>Clase BCN</u>, 2007

The Catalan chef Carles Abellán opened his first own restaurant at Carrer Comerç number 24. A catering service and two further restaurants followed, all subsumed under the heading Project 24 and Abellán's dedication to fine cuisine in contemporary settings at reasonable prices.

One of Carles Abellán's restaurants is Tapas, 24. The décor is that of a typical tapas bar—the menus on each table are written on little black chalkboards. Drawing heavily on traditional tapas bar aesthetics, Clase BCN developed a rustic brand image—but with a range of playful letterings, illustrative elements, and a contemporary twist.

174

"The identity is a tapa style selection of type, pictogramms, icons, and illustrations, linked with the image of the typical Tapas bar from Barceloneta."

moomah   moomah   moomah

Moomah

New York City, USA

Apartment One, 2010

Moomah is a creative playspace, a cozy café, a living classroom, a quiet hideaway, an art oasis, and a neighborhood meeting spot. Tracey Stewart set it up as a place where imagination is king, where parents are inspired by their children, and teach them that anything is pos-

"A place of sweet whimsy, wonder and warmth, Moomah is a creative playspace, a cozy café, a living classroom, a quiet hideaway, an art oasis, your neighborhood meeting spot. Your favorite place to be together, and a place for your child to simply be."

sible. Envisioning a brand language that would communicate her ideals, she approached Apartment One. The designers came up with a lively solution that guarantees a strong brand image without feeling too corporate. Three different variations of the M illustrate the core brand values. A range of application-specific, dreamlike illustrations pass Moomah's phantasmagorical spirit on to stationery, cups, bags, and stickers.

Coffee & Kitchen

Graz, Austria

<u>**Moodley Brand Identity**</u>, 2011

Situated in a busy business district of Graz, the new Coffee & Kitchen restaurant brings culinary pleasure into its clientele's nine-to-five lifestyle.

Moodley Brand Identity's branding strategy combines plain black-and-white elements with natural colors and the wooden furniture used for the restaurant's interior to create a minimal yet homely and welcoming atmosphere. To give the eyes of Coffee & Kitchen customers a break from the usual information overload, all printed material is deliberately left unbranded—only a range of logo stickers signalize the product's identity. Handwritten typography supports a relaxed and informal restaurant atmosphere.

le Petit Canon

Cocktails

COSMOPOLITAN	7,50
(Vodka, Cointreau, jus de citron, jus d'airelle)	
MARGARITA	7,50
(Tequila, Cointreau, citron)	
CUBA LIBRE	7,50
(Rhum brun, Cola, citron vert)	
WHISKY SOUR	7,50
(Jack Daniels, citron, sucre de canne)	
BLOODY MARY	7,50
(Vodka, citron, jus de tomate)	

Les Bulles

KIR ROYAL	8,50
COUPE DE	
. CHAMPAGNE 'BERGÈRE'	7,50
. CAVA BRUT 'PALAU'	5,80
. 1ères BULLES DE LIMOUX	5,80
BOUTEILLE DE	
. CHAMPAGNE 'BERGÈRE'	45,00
. CAVA BRUT 'PALAU'	29,00
. 1ères BULLES DE LIMOUX	29,00

Apéritifs

KIR	4,00
PORTO	4,00
SHERRY	4,00
MARTINI	4,00
CAMPARI	4,00
PASTIS	4,00

Alcools & Liqueurs
(accompagnement soft + 2,00)

BOMBAY SAPHIRE	6,00
GORDON'S	5,00
ABSOLUT	5,00
JB	
CHIV	
GLEN	
JACK	
HAV	
HAV	
LIMO	
AMA	
GRA	
MOS	

Biè

SUPE	
*(dans	
JUPIL	
BLAN	
KRIE	
DUV	
TRIPI	

LES PETITS CANONS

NOS SUGGESTIONS DE
D

— To

Boissons fraîches

THÉ GLACÉ MAISON	2,50
CAFÉ GLACÉ MAISON	2,50
LE LAZARDO	2,90
(jus de gingembre frais)	
JUS FRAIS	3,70
(orange, pamplemousse, citron)	

MENU

Le Midi

BAGNATS*
Servis avec une petite salade

*CREVETTES GRISES	
Tomate, Roquette	5,50
*CLUB / Jambon, Fromage, Oeufs	
Tomate, Salade, Mayonnaise	4,60
*SAUMON FUMÉ / Crème épaisse,	
Ciboulette, Roquette	5,10
SOUPE DU JOUR	
(servie avec pain et beurre)	4,00
QUICHE DU JOUR (servie avec	
une petite salade)	6,50

Mises en bouche

SALADE WAKAME AU SÉSAME	4,60
SALADE DE LENTILLES	3,90
CROQUE MONSIEUR	4,00
SALADE DE BETTERAVES ROUGES ET ROQUETTE	3,90
ASSIETTE DE CHARCUTERIE	6,50

Le Goûter

TARTE DU JOUR	5,00
FRUIT DE SAISON	1,00
CROQUE MELO	
Fromage, Banane, Miel	3,00
FONDANT AU CHOCOLAT	
avec glace vanille bourbon	6,50
PASTEL DE NATA	1,80

ASSIETTE DE FROMAGE	7,00
ASSORTIMENT DE CHORIZOS PORTUGAIS CHAUDS	4,50
RILLETTE DU MANS	4,00
JAMBON SERRANO, PAIN FROTTÉ À L'AIL ET TOMATE	4,90
PÂTÉ DE CAMPAGNE	4,00

Zakouskis

PISTACHES	1,00
OLIVES	1,50
LUPINS	1,50
ANCHOIS MARINÉS	2,00
POULPES MARINÉS	2,50

Nos Conserves
(servies avec du pain, ½ citron, fleur de sel et poivre noir)

SARDINES À L'HUILE D'OLIVE	4,20
FOIE DE MORUE	4,20
CALAMARES	4,20
THON AU NATUREL	4,20

OEUF MAYONNAISE	1,50
TOAST DE MÉMÉ AU FROMAGE	4,00
BLINIS AU SAUMON FUMÉ, CRÈME ÉPAISSE À LA CIBOULETTE	4,90
TRIO DE TAPENADES SERVIS AVEC DES GRISSINI	4,50

— Consultez également notre tableau de suggestions —

le Petit Canon

BISTRO . BAR À VIN . MISES EN BOUCHE

le Petit Canon
91 rue Lesbroussart
1050 Bruxelles

Ouvert tous les jours
de 12h00 à 22h00
Fermé le dimanche

t. **02 640 38 34**
lpc@lepetitcanon.be
www.lepetitcanon.be

Agenda des soirées sur facebook

Le Petit Canon

Brussels, Belgium

Codefrisko, 2009

Le Petit Canon is a bar and restaurant offering excellent vintage wines alongside quiches, soups, and pan bagnats in a retro bistro setting. The old-fashioned French expression *le petit canon* has two idiomatic meanings: small glass of wine and gorgeous girl. Commissioned with the development of the brand's identity, Codefrisko took inspiration from both meanings, as well as from the somewhat dated feel of the expression.

Cava
Toronto, Canada

Concrete, 2006

In Spanish, *cava* means both wine cellar and Catalan sparkling white wine. It is also the name of Toronto chef Chris McDonald's wine and tapas bar. The restaurant's food combines culinary influences of Spain, Italy, and France with occasional Mexican flourishes. One of the core values is chef McDonald's in-house cured meat that served as an inspiration for the whimsical illustrations at the heart of Concrete's otherwise rustic visual identity.

PanPan
Atelier

Valencia, Spain

Rocío Martinavarro, 2010

The PanPan Atelier is a local bakery chain offering regional varieties of Spanish bread. Founded in 2008 by Daniel Martinavarro, it now has five branches across the city of Valencia.

Keen to keep things in the family, Martinavarro asked his sister Rocío to design the branding for his business. Her solution celebrates the main ingredient of the company's primary product: Simplified wheat ears form a chevron pattern reminiscent of the antique esparto baskets, in which bread used to be displayed in traditional bakeries. The company's name is set in custom-made letters and links up the Spanish word *pan* for bread with the expression *nam nam* (yum yum). Word repetition is used to express authenticity. Bread-bread = real bread. The concept of repetition becomes a recurrent theme of PanPan's identity and is taken up by its slogan: "PanPan. Repetirás" (BreadBread. You will repeat).

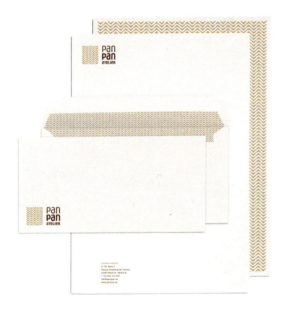

**Lento leeento.
Sin prisas.
Así es el proceso
de elaboración del
auténtico pan.**
PANPAN. Repetirás

pan
pan
ATELIER®

Nolitan

New York City, USA

<u>Marque</u>, 2010

For those who like to be based in Nolita, "North of Little Italy" when in New York City, the Nolitan Hotel is just the thing. At the corner of Kenmare and Elizabeth Streets, it is the first luxury boutique hotel in Manhattan to open in this area. Marque created the name, positioning, brand identity, signage and way finding, as well as toiletries, in-room materials, a Nolitan brand newspaper and all marketing materials for the hotel. The warm and friendly look of the brand celebrates the diversity of the neighborhood and the local niche businesses that make Nolita so unique, encouraging guests to become a Nolitan, too.

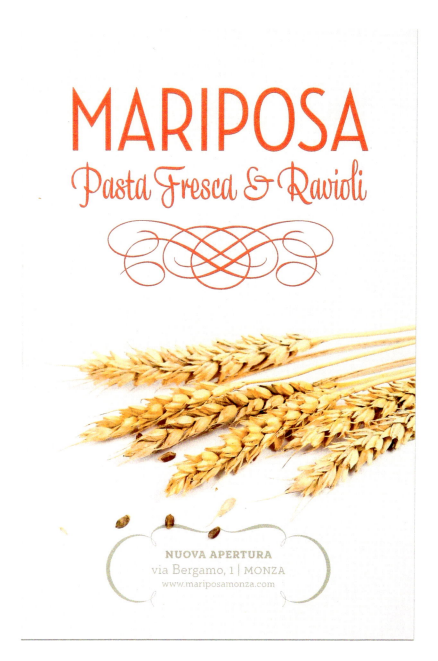

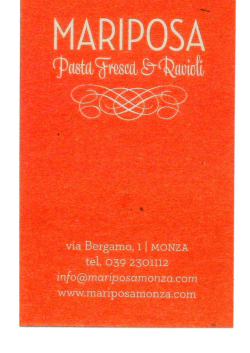

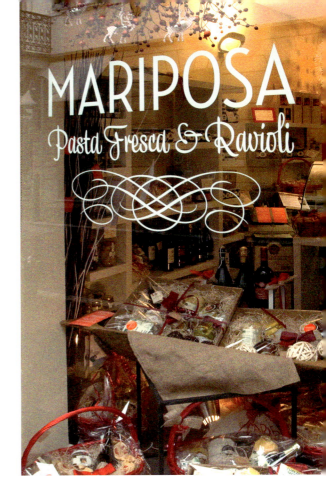

Mariposa

Monza, Italy

La Tigre, 2010

Mariposa is a small pasta shop offering handmade fresh noodles and a lovingly selected range of regional fine foods. Adapting the visual language of historical food packaging, La Tigre designed a traditional, homey, yet quirkily distinct identity that references Mariposa's original production process.

Manifesto

New York City, USA

The Bear Cave, 2011

Derived from the Latin word *manifestum,* Manifesto means clear or conspicuous and Manifesto Film Production

seems to identify with this original meaning. The visual identity by The Bear Cave bridges the gap between simple modernist shapes and grandiose nostalgia, a response to slick and over-designed branding, the kind that tends to follow current trends and becomes passé a year later.

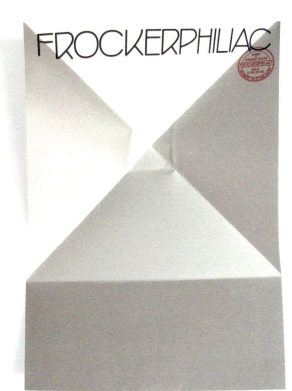

> "Frockerphiliac is a styling service with a personal touch and a sustainable bent. Single items of collateral serve multiple functions cutting down on waste and touching on the business' sustainable practice."

Frockerphiliac

Melbourne, Australia

A Friend of Mine, 2009

Kim Kneipp studied fashion design in Sydney before embarking on a frock career in Melbourne, where amongst other things, she developed products for major department chains. Under the label Frockerphiliac she now works as an independent sustainable designer, personal stylist, and workshop facilitator. The mission to resurrect and refit old wardrobe pieces in an environmentally conscious styling process is reflected by a brand image that speaks the visual language of long bygone decades. A Friend of Mine introduced art nouveau lettering, a rhombic emblem, and added Alphons Mucha-like illustrations. To support the core value of eco-friendly styling, all branding elements have been developed to serve multiple functions. Rather than defining a fixed range of communication materials, A Friend of Mine created a flexible and resourceful branding system that consists of a set of customized stickers, rubber stamps, postcards, folding techniques, and red ribbon.

Morton & Peplow

Munich, Germany

Magpie Studio, 2007

Morton & Peplow is a Munich-based delicatessen shop that specializes in British cuisine. Asked to develop the brand's identity, Magpie Studio combined two icons of Britishness—the bowler hat and the domed silver service platter—creating a brand mark that evokes a sense of heritage and style. A candy color palette and classic typography reinforce this quintessentially British feel, tipping its hat to a lost era of elegant simplicity.

Frøystad+ Klock

Oslo, Norway

Heydays, 2010

A joint passion for problem solving, experimenting and design underlies the work of Frøystad+Klock, a furniture studio operating from an old workshop space in Oslo's city center.

Inspired by Scandinavian design traditions and Frøystad+ Klock's appreciation of pure materials, Heydays developed a stripped down, minimalistic graphic identity. The designers focused on typographic subtleties of the word mark and combined it with twelve different pattern structures based on photographic reproductions of Frøystad+Klock's basic materials. The stationery is printed on two kinds of colored paper stock — one for Frøystad, one for Klock.

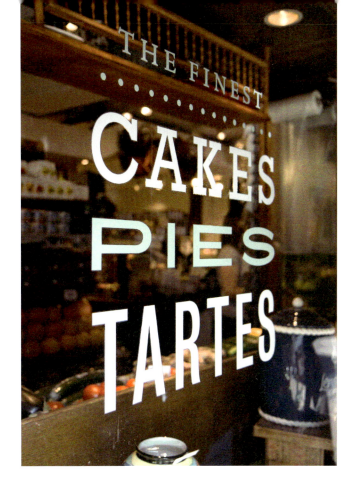

Butterfield Market

New York, USA

<u>Mucca Design</u>, 2007

enterprise from a local phenomenon to a widely recognized food retailer and with it the need for a professional, cohesive identity. Commissioned with the development of the Butterfield Market brand, Mucca Design came up with a scripty B-monogram, a

Butterfield Market is a family-owned gourmet grocery and an institution in New York's Upper East Side neighborhood. With the addition of a new catering division came the growth of the

range of illustrations in the style of traditional engravings, and an overall visual language that embraces the family business's heritage by creating a warm and personal atmosphere.

Le Buro
Bulle, Switzerland

Inventaire, 2010 (ongoing)

Le Buro is a bar and restaurant. With the aim of sparking the curiosity of a diverse clientele, Inventaire combined the venue's early twentieth-century structure with a sober visual identity. Straight architectural lines meet vivid colors and massive typographic compositions.

Silver Lining

New York City, USA

GrandArmy, 2010

Silver Lining Opticians is the joint venture of Erik Sacher, a licensed optician, and Jordan Silver, a vintage eyewear purveyor. Addressing the discerning shopper who seeks the highest level of quality and service, Sacher and Silver curate a selection of independent contemporary and vintage eyewear and the largest unused vintage collection in New York. The merging of the old and the new is reflected in the store's interior and contrasted with a more timeless graphic identity by GrandArmy.

"Our experience is unique—we curate a selection of independent contemporary brands with the largest unused vintage eyewear collection in New York. We are the only store declining to sell any licensed brands which dominate the market. Working with factories in Europe and drawing on our vast vintage for inspiration, we have launched our own eponymous line."

Ambrose

Montreal, Canada

Kissmiklos, 2011

Ambrose is a little hotel in Montreal, with rooms across two Victorian-style buildings. Inspired by the history of the hotel's premises, Kissmiklos drew the scripty logo lettering by hand and refined the letterforms with reference to the typical typefaces of the Victorian era. The extensive black-and-white identity includes wine labels, "clean room please" signs, room numbers, pencils, and stationery.

The Glass House

Montreal, Canada

Catherine Bourdon, 2010

The Glass House is a restaurant, bar, and venue specialized in homemade beers, snacks, and live music. Responding to the limitations of a tight budget, Catherine Bourdon created a one-color identity that is simple but certainly distinctive. A bit of grit and copy machine imperfections contrast the iconographic simplicity and reflect the venue's punk and hardcore roots. All branded materials are printed using vegetable-based black ink on colored Bier Lager card stock.

OzCo Williams

Brisbane, Australia

Cheyanne, 2010

OzCo Williams is a cinema advertising company that helps local businesses get their name up on the big screen. Working with over twenty selected cinemas, the small company brings together all the necessary ingredients, prepares everything for the client, and then makes big things happen. Taking inspiration from cooking, film, and newspaper classifieds, Cheyanne Proud's identity solution presents cinema advertising as every business's cup of tea: A significant, powerful, yet affordable tool of corporate communication.

Supporting badges for the different disciplines of Tom, Dick & Harry

Tom, Dick & Harry

Chicago, USA

McQuade, 2011

The graphic design and advertising agency Tom, Dick & Harry decided not to do their branding themselves but to entrust Mike McQuade with the task. To create the industrial look his colleagues strived for, McQuade brought sign painter Stephen Reynolds in to paint the logo and script letterings that form the basis of the corporate identity. The rest he did himself.

Percy & Reed

London, UK

Everyone Associates, 2007

Having spent decades tending to the locks of the rich and famous, the two hairdressers Paul Percival and Adam Reed decided to tend to their own business: Percy & Reed, a classic British salon with a contemporary twist. They commissioned Everyone Associates to create a brand image that would suggest both modernity and traditional British craftsmanship.

The result is an eclectic mix of old and new: The logo is inspired by the original Victorian shop front of Percy & Reed's premises and references the traditional tools of the trade. Clean type is contrasted by a distinctive ampersand, reminiscent of a lock of hair. Each staff member has a suite of business cards in different colorways; the color palette references the interior of the salon. Foil blocking, blind embossing and duplexing imply premium quality, the overall fresh and friendly tone suggest fashionable style and customer proximity.

With a Twist

The carpenter, the model agent, the emergency electrician, and the deli corner shop—sectors and businesses all across the spectrum are afflicted by harsh market conditions and mushrooming competitors. The pressure to succeed grows, especially for small enterprises that start out on a slender budget. There are two particularly effective survival strategies: to work in an economically efficient way and to stand out from the crowd.

The conceptual approaches featured in this section are designed to perform very specific but essentially different tasks. Many focus on the development of highly efficient corporate tools and their effective application. Others count on uniqueness, on a peculiar—sometimes even perplexing—visual presentation that deliberately clashes with the conventions of the business sector. Some are a combination of both. They all have an agenda—only the items on it differ.

There are clever sets of branding devices that enable small businesses to make the most of their limited budgets. The designers of Unreal, for example, equipped the People's Supermarket ◆ p. 226 with a hole punch in shape of a Euroslot—the small hole at the top of packaging normally used to hang the product up on display stands—and thus with a cost effective, easy-to-use design tool which can give a unique touch to anything from letterheads to carrier bags and wine labels. Our Polite Society developed a clever all-in-one identity solution for the industrial designer Doreen Westphal: ◆ p. 236 a perforated printing sheet that is divided into various units to be used as business cards, product cards, and hang tags.

There are sets of mix and match design elements that allow for maximum flexibility and a variety of cost efficient corporate material. Lundgren+Lindquist's business cards for the photographer Cora Hillebrand, ◆ p. 239 for example, are flexible combinations of photos and envelope-like wrappers that enable the artist to update her cards in accordance with her expanding portfolio and to adjust them to particular client needs.

There is unorthodox symbolism, off-the-wall material, and unexpected visual language that attracts a great deal of attention without boosting expenses. Pirol present Stefan Reinhardt's one-man-business for de-escalation using a series of photographs of erupting volcanoes, ◆ p. 220 Julian Zimmermann designs the car mechanic König Bansah's ◆ p. 206 identity in close reference to the entrepreneur's royal descent. Attack use Gaffa tape, a simple, elementary tool of the film industry, to create a unique and memorable corporate image for the Ghetto Film School, ◆ p. 246 and Pam&Jenny appoint a pack of porcelain dogs from flea markets as brand mascots for the Kaki Restaurant. ◆ p. 248

Loosely connected through their lateral approaches, this section may seem uneven and slightly inconsistent. Maybe that is because out-of-the-box concepts simply cannot be neatly packaged.

U R K U N D E

~~~~~~~~~~~~~~~~~~

IN ANERKENNUNG UND WÜRDIGUNG BESONDERER ZUWENDUNGEN UND HILFEN
FÜR DAS KÖNIGREICH VON HOHOE GHANA WIRD HIERMIT ALS DANK DES VOLKES
DURCH SEINEN KÖNIG

KÖNIG BANSAH

TOGBUI NGORYIFIA CÉPHAS KOSI BANSAH
KÖNIG VON HOHOE GBI TRADITIONAL GHANA

DIESE URKUNDE VERLIEHEN AN

_____

KÖNIGLICHE UNTERSCHRIFT   KÖNIGLICHES SIEGEL

TOGBUI NGORYIFIA KOSI CÉPHAS BANSAH
KÖNIG VON HOHOE GBI TRADITIONAL GHANA

König Bansah

Ludwigshafen, Germany

Deutsche & Japaner, 2010

The African King Bansah lives and works as a car mechanic in Ludwigshafen and governs his people from there. As a singer, frequent guest in TV shows, initiator of diverse charity events, and with his own royal brewery he raises money for a number of aid projects.

A combination of royal and exotic impressions, King Bansah's corporate design pays tribute to his regal African background and suggests authenticity and lordliness.

The logo is based on the royal emblem of King Bansah's family and incorporates the edged and primal shapes of the woven clothes of the Ewe people. Golden hot foil embossing on black and chamois-colored uncoated paper express the exotic and royal flair of both King Bansah himself and his rather unconventional business.

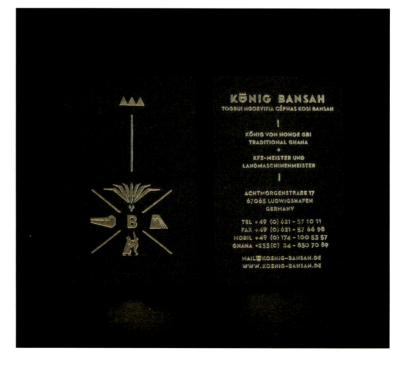

The Den is a bar located in the basement level of The Atlantic Restaurant in Melbourne's Crown Entertainment Complex. Designed to feel like a vintage gentlemen's lounge, its visual identity is a playful interpretation of this atmosphere. Poking fun at the formal tone of the environment and the seafood consumption in the restaurant above, the designers of 21-19 developed a brand image based on a series of surreal "portraits."

THE DEN

AT THE ATLANTIC

Alison Tickner
Managing Director

m 07702 291082
e alison@gardenlighting.co.uk

Garden Lighting Company
The Croft Haslingden Road Rawtenstall Lancashire BB4 6RE
t +44(0)1706 227525 f +44(0)1706 227525
e info@gardenlighting.co.uk www.gardenlighting.co.uk

Garden Lighting Company
The Croft Haslingden Road Rawtenstall Lancashire BB4 6RE
t +44(0)1706 227525 f +44(0)1706 227525
e info@gardenlighting.co.uk www.gardenlighting.co.uk

Laura Mackenzie
Business Development Consultant

t +44(0)1706 227525
e laura@gardenlighting.co.uk

Garden Lighting Company
The Croft Haslingden Road Rawtenstall Lancashire BB4 6RE
t +44(0)1706 227525 f +44(0)1706 227525
e info@gardenlighting.co.uk www.gardenlighting.co.uk

Garden Lighting Company
The Croft Haslingden Road Rawtenstall Lancashire BB4 6RE
t +44(0)1706 227525 f +44(0)1706 227525
e info@gardenlighting.co.uk www.gardenlighting.co.uk

Garden Lighting Company

Rawtenstall, UK

The Chase, 2006

Based in a small town at the center of the Rossendale Valley in Lancashire, the Garden Lighting Company offers decorative and security lighting for outdoors. The Chase created a set of stationery that is striking in its beautiful simplicity—both in terms of the idea and its visual representation.

Alison Tickner
Managing Director

m 07702 291082
e alison@gardenlighting.co.uk

Garden Lighting Company
The Croft Haslingden Road Rawtenstall Lancashire BB4 6RE
t +44(0)1706 227525 f +44(0)1706 227525
e info@gardenlighting.co.uk www.gardenlighting.co.uk

Garden Lighting Company
The Croft Haslingden Road Rawtenstall Lancashire BB4 6RE
t +44(0)1706 227525 f +44(0)1706 227525
e info@gardenlighting.co.uk www.gardenlighting.co.uk

Laura Mackenzie
Business Development Consultant

t +44(0)1706 227525
e laura@gardenlighting.co.uk

Garden Lighting Company
The Croft Haslingden Road Rawtenstall Lancashire BB4 6RE
t +44(0)1706 227525 f +44(0)1706 227525
e info@gardenlighting.co.uk www.gardenlighting.co.uk

Garden Lighting Company
The Croft Haslingden Road Rawtenstall Lancashire BB4 6RE
t +44(0)1706 227525 f +44(0)1706 227525
e info@gardenlighting.co.uk www.gardenlighting.co.uk

Union

Brighton, UK

Red Design, 2011

The Union jewelry store is located on Union Street in Brighton, in the heart of The Lanes, a bustling pedestrian area full of eclectic places to shop and eat. Both in store and online, Union offers a fine selection of fashion and costume jewelry, as well as a bridal jewelry service.

Commissioned with the development of Union's corporate identity, Red Design created a custom Union lettering and an illustrative emblem based on the initial U, used to accompany the word mark if space and applications allow, and to mark the pieces of Union's own jewelry range.

The four rings of the emblem reference the concept of union and, however obliquely, the atomic structure of jewelry and the four mythical elements required to produce it—earth, fire, water, and air. Derived from the U emblem is a modular graphic element that can appear in a variety of different colorways loosely defined by the identity's extensive palette of bold tones and graduated tints.

Carla
Melbourne, Australia

A Friend of Mine, 2010

Carla Grbac weaves pieces of clothing, accessories, and jewelry and aptly describes herself as "a maker of things." Creating an identity for Carla, A Friend of Mine focused on referencing the traditional process of her work, in which rows of thread are woven around the reeds of a large loom. The result is a monochromatic visual language, and geometric patterns that create a certain op-art feel. The use of textural production techniques references the tactile nature of Carla's work.

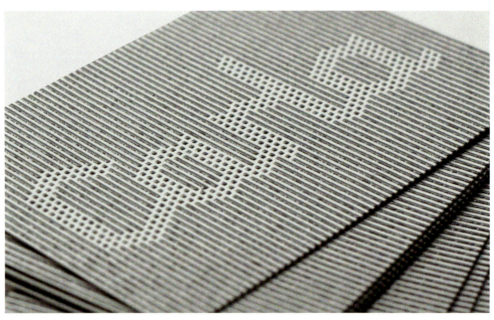

"A bold monochromatic identity that has an op-art quality and weaving diagram sensibility."

H.E.R.O.

London, UK

D.Studio, 2010

The Hong Kong Escape Re-enactment Organisation (H.E.R.O.) was formed to commemorate and raise awareness of the great escape of the 2nd MTB flotilla and VIP party from Hong Kong to freedom in China on Christmas Day, 1941. H.E.R.O.'s founders, all descendants of the real life heroes involved in the escape, asked D.Studio to create a graphic identity that would not only arouse the interest of potential sponsors for the organization but also inform them, bit by bit, of the heroic story it aims to spotlight.

D.Studio designed a set of business cards in the style of collectible cigarette cards, each portraying a relative of the organization's founding members. As well as being an integral part of the new corporate image, these cards provided fresh talking points at meetings and thus raised internal communication to another level. To enhance the external brand presence of the organization, D.Studio replicated an official 1940s letter that appeared to have been lost in the post for decades, complete with postmark style identity and a censor seal for added authenticity. Inside was a telegram-style letter detailing H.E.R.O's "mission," complete with a map of the escape route.

You
Stockholm

Stockholm, Sweden

25AH Design Studio, 2010

"We always strive to be a creative, feel good space for all involved with us."

Established and run by the renowned stylist Steve Terry & his
wife Helene, You Stockholm is
a hairdressing salon and a dynamic hub of creativity. Inspired
by Steve's charming personality and his passionate, loving
approach to hairdressing 25AH
decided to go for a very warm
and personal corporate image.
The core mission is to make
the customer feel cared for and
comfortable.

Stefan Reinhardt

Zurich, Switzerland

Pirol, 2011

Stefan Reinhardt practices professional de-escalation. A large part of his clientele are expert personnel from the healthcare sector and social services, for whom he offers consulting, training courses, and workshops in aggression management to facilitate the interaction with violent patients. In view of his highly defined, specialized client base, Reinhardt agreed to a fairly unconventional way of communicating his business: Pirol thought laterally and approached the subject matter by means of rather drastic symbolism. Photos of smoking volcanoes cover postcards, business cards, and stationery, and function as oblique hints to one of the key aspects of Reinhardt's services: early recognition of the patients' potential for aggression.

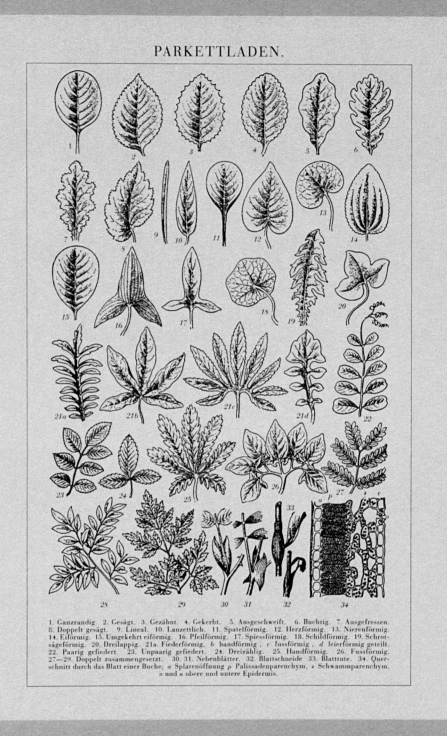

PARKETTLADEN.

Parkettladen

Zurich, Switzerland

Esther Rieser, 2007

The Parkettladen—German for parquet store—distributes high-quality flooring. The visual identity of the small Zurich-based business is as straightforward and unpretentious as its name. Down-to-earth typography and a plain logo reflect the elementary, artless nature of the product. The overall simplicity is contrasted with elaborate illustrations in the style of traditional etchings, visual expressions of durability, and precise craftsmanship.

Dan Syrový

Prague, Czech Republic

Touch, 2010

Dan Syrový is a one-man business specializing in text-based brand consultancy. Syrový
asked Touch to create a unique image that
would communicate himself as a brand and
his services to the client.

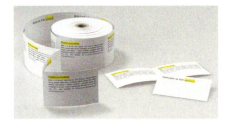

Inspired by their client's name and the
characteristics of his work, the designers
came up with an identity that not only bor-
rows the look of word processing software,
but was in fact entirely composed in Text
Edit. Setting aside the conventional designer's toolkit, Touch played on linguistic am-
biguity: *Syrový* means "raw" or "rough" in
Czech, which happens to be an apt description of the brand consultant's personal style
of work. As suggested by his set of business
cards ("Bringing you rough ideas," "I promise to be rough on you," "I'm not afraid to be
rough"), Syrový delivers straightforward, raw
ideas to his clients.

Přinášim *syrový* nápady.

Mūžu si to dovolit. Jsem Syrový. Dan Syrový. Nemám žádnou
funkci, protože žádná funkce nezahrnuje vše co přinesu Vaší značce.
Hledám malé příčiny s velkými následky a přinášim nápady pro
nadnárodní korporace i rodinné společnosti. Dovoláte se mi na 603
554 071, nebo emailujte na daniel.syrovy@centrum.cz.
www.dansyrovy.cz

Přinášim *syrový* nápady.

Nebojím se být *syrový.*

Hledáte *syrový* nápady?

Když mluvím,
tak jsem syrový.

The People's Supermarket

London, UK

Unreal, 2010

The People's Supermarket is a brand new not-for-profit co-operative grocery offering communal, affordable food at a reasonable price. Set up by chef Arthur Potts-Dawson and his co-founder Kate Bull, it is billed as an antidote to larger, profit-hungry supermarket chains, and acts as a community-based shop managed and owned by voluntary members. To support their vision of a communal, affordable, and democratic shopping experience, Potts-Dawson and Bull commissioned Unreal with the development of a clever and cost-effective branding strategy.

In their search for ideas, the designers stumbled upon the Euroslot, a largely unnoticed symbol of the trade. Since much of the packaging and print material has to be produced in store by the volunteers, a Euroslot punch was acquired to serve as an easy to implement, cost effective solution for a distinct design: Cutting easily through anything from letterheads to in-store packaging, the clever branding device became the key design element across all communications.

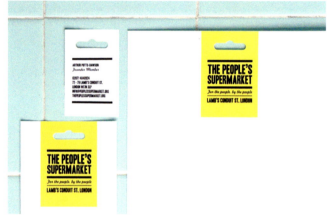

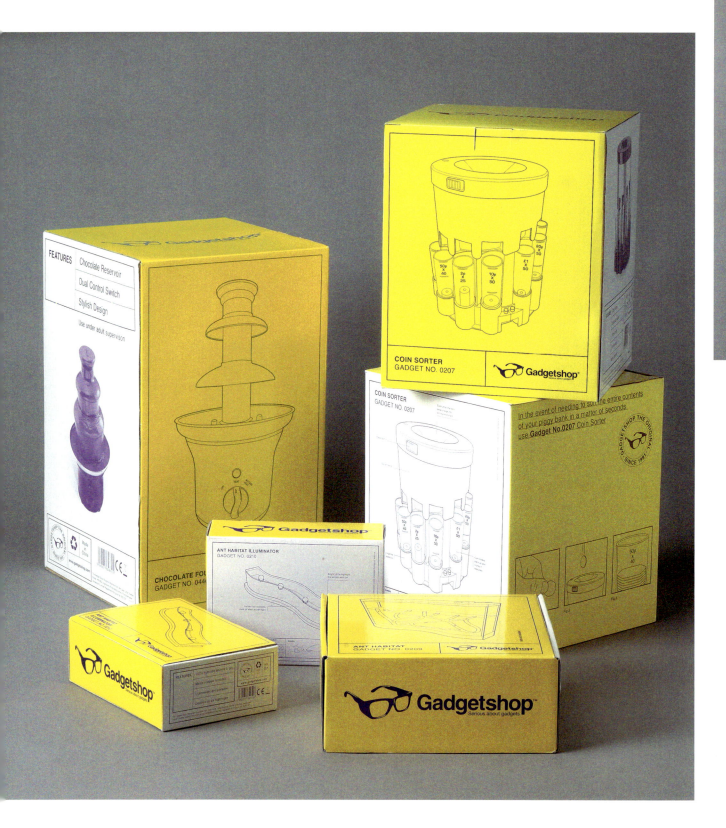

Gadgetshop

London, UK

**ArthurSteenHorneAdamson
(ASHA), 2008**

The Gadgetshop is "serious about gadgets" and that is what distinguishes it from its competitors.

When relaunched under new ownership, ASHA developed a branding strategy based on this premise. Inspired by James Bond and "M," the designers focused on individual features and the science behind each gadget, and linked each product to a specific mission and technical illustration.

A wittily implemented store design, advertising, and a new catalogue and website supported the repositioning of existing products. The Gadgetshop's relaunch was followed by steady growth, and the company was acquired by WHSmith in September 2010.

Mirror
Shine
Valets

Edinburgh, Scotland

Tayburn, 2011

Mirror Shine Valets clean cars.
Commissioned to heighten the
visibility of the small business

and communicate it as a brand,
Tyburn came up with a business card that could be left on
the dashboard of a vehicle and
would be memorable, unique,
and therefore kept by the recipi-
ent: a piece of dry sponge with
waterproof screen-printed type
on it.

*"Just add water.

MIRROR SHINE VALETS
Matt Smith
Gifford House, Main Street, West Linton EH46 7EE
T. 07515 674 955 E. msvalets@yahoo.co.uk
www.mirrorshinevalets.co.uk

JESSIE
0773-691-1112

Jessica Owen - dog & cat sitting
St Bernards Crescent Stockbridge
jessica.owen@gmail.com

Jessica Owen

Edinburgh, Scotland

Tayburn, 2011

Jessica Owen works as a dog walker and cat sitter in Edinburgh. Wishing to add a distinct and professional look to her little business, she approached Tyburn, who created a rather unconventional set of business cards: Imitating the size, shape, material, and typeset of pet tags, Jessica's contact details can potentially be tied to her animal clients' collars.

Dr. Thomas Shaw

Edinburgh, Scotland

Tayburn, 2010

Dr. Thomas Shaw Bsc, MD, FRCP, FESC, is an experienced cardiologist, an Honorary Consultant at the Royal Infirmary of Edinburgh and an Honorary Senior Lecturer at the University of Edinburgh. Tyburn interpreted Dr. Shaw's area of medical expertise symbolically to create a unique set of business cards. His details are screen printed onto 52 vintage "ace of hearts" playing cards, nicely packaged in a typical card box. He is probably the only doctor who introduces himself by getting out a card deck.

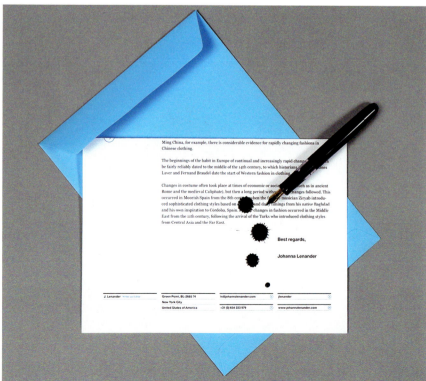

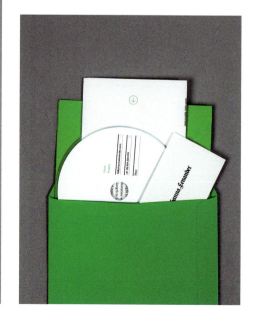

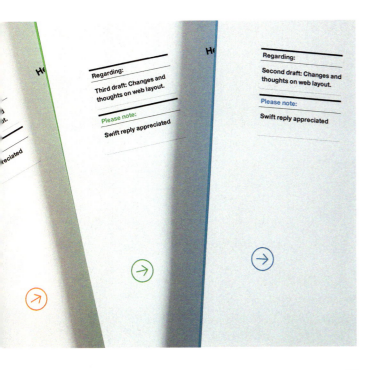

Johanna Lenander

New York City, USA

Lundgren+Lindqvist, 2010

Johanna Lenander is a writer and editor, living and working in New York City. With a prestigious client list that includes the *New York Times* style magazine, *Elle*, Gucci, and Karl Lagerfeld, Johanna needed an identity that would not only dis-

play her writing skills but also reflect her sense of style. Lundgren+Lindqvist came up with an aesthetic that follows the editorial tradition of classic newspapers, but with a modern twist, a special touch, and nice little extras such as relief printing and fluorescent ink.

WESTERDOK 780
1013BV AMSTERDAM
THE NETHERLANDS

DOREEN WESTPHAL STUDIO
+31 (0)6 24 240 989 CONTACT@DOREENWESTPHAL.COM WWW.DOREENWESTPHAL.COM

WESTPHAL

DOREEN   STUDIO WESTERDOK 780 1013BV AMSTERDAM THE NETHERLANDS
+31 (0)6 24 240 989 CONTACT@DOREENWESTPHAL.COM WWW.DOREENWESTPHAL.COM

STUDIO

DOREEN WESTPHAL   WESTERDOK 780 1013BV AMSTERDAM THE NETHERLANDS
+31 (0)6 24 240 989 CONTACT@DOREENWESTPHAL.COM WWW.DOREENWESTPHAL.COM

DOREEN

WESTPHAL STUDIO WESTERDOK 780 1013BV AMSTERDAM THE NETHERLANDS
+31 (0)6 24 240 989 CONTACT@DOREENWESTPHAL.COM WWW.DOREENWESTPHAL.COM

+31 (0)6 24 240 989

DOREEN WESTPHAL STUDIO WESTERDOK 780 1013BV AMSTERDAM THE NETHERLANDS
CONTACT@DOREENWESTPHAL.COM WWW.DOREENWESTPHAL.COM

CONTACT@DOREENWESTPHAL.COM

DOREEN WESTPHAL STUDIO WESTERDOK 780 1013BV AMSTERDAM THE NETHERLANDS
+31 (0)6 24 240 989   WWW.DOREENWESTPHAL.COM

WWW.DOREENWESTPHAL.COM

DOREEN WESTPHAL STUDIO WESTERDOK 780 1013BV AMSTERDAM THE NETHERLANDS
+31 (0)6 24 240 989 CONTACT@DOREENWESTPHAL.COM

DOREEN WESTPHAL STUDIO WESTERDOK 780 1013BV AMSTERDAM THE NETHERLANDS
+31 (0)6 24 240 989 CONTACT@DOREENWESTPHAL.COM WWW.DOREENWESTPHAL.COM

Doreen Westphal

Amsterdam, Netherlands

Our Polite Society, 2010

Doreen Westphal is an industrial designer and a tailor by trade. After studying theater design in the UK, she moved to Amsterdam to establish her own little business. Since then, Doreen Westphal stands for handmade, high-quality finished products, the innovative combination of purposeful design, original materials, and a production process that is conscious of social and environmental issues.

Since Westphal works mainly as a self producing designer in her own workshop, Our Polite Society provided her with a clever piece of brand identity that she can process herself: a perforated printing sheet, divided into various units to be used for different purposes, such as business cards, letterhead, product cards, hang tags, etc.

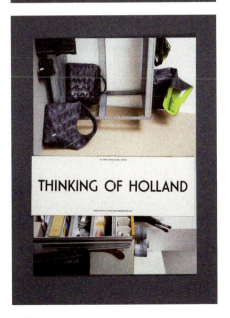

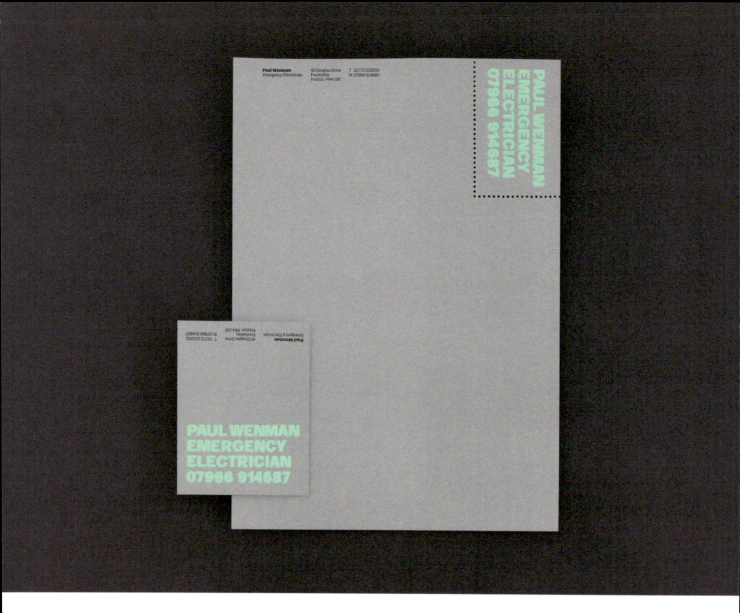

Paul
Wenman

Freckleton, UK

The Chase, 2008

Paul Wenman works as an emergency electrician in a village called Frackleton on the Fylde coast in Lancashire. The Chase created a stationery range that ensures his customers will never be without Paul when they need him the most.

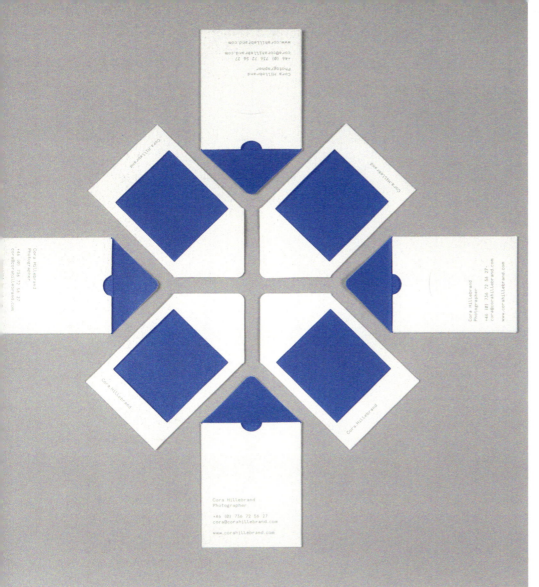

Cora Hillebrandt

Gothenburg, Sweden

Lundgren+Lindqvist, 2011

Cora Hillebrandt is a photographer. As she often has to carry heavy equipment, she wanted a clever piece of brand identity that she could easily carry with her and leave with clients. The solution was a combined business card and mini portfolio. Lundgren+Lindqvist designed a sturdy envelope in the shape of a Polaroid picture with an open front. Nine images from different projects by the artist were printed on cardboard and perforated for easy detachment. This enables Cora to compose various mini portfolios customized for different client types. Pre-perforated printer-friendly paper allows for quick updates.

needed to suggest: technical formality and the highest cinematographic quality. The designers decided to add visual references to Nemesis's scarcity value as one of the first horror-film production companies in Latin America. Drawing inspiration from ancient runes, they created a graphic atmosphere of magic and rituals. The complexity of the monogram is contrasted with the clean lines of the type.

NEMESIS FILMS,
—VICTOR DRYERE, PRODUCER
DRYERE@NEMESISNEMESIS.COM
+ 52 (81) 1255.0397
NEMESISNEMESIS.COM

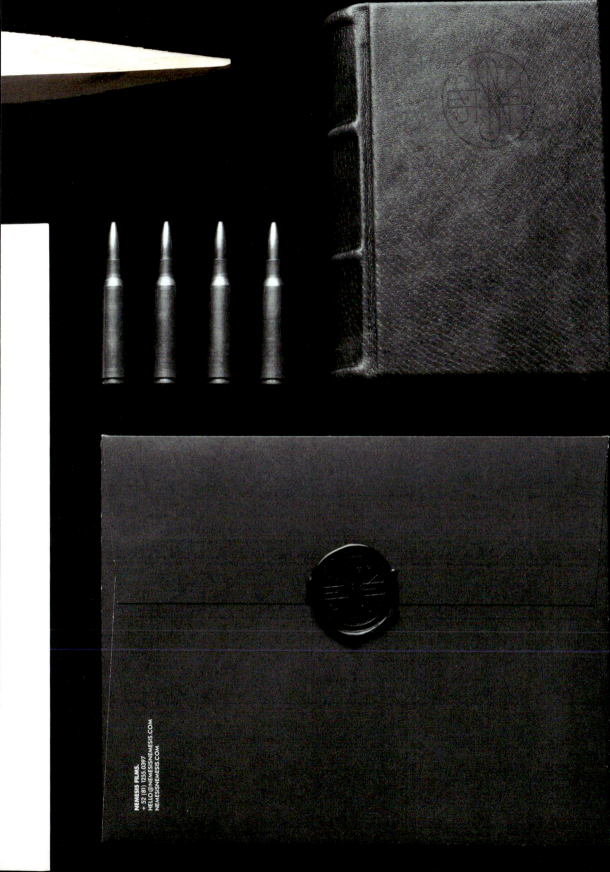

NEMESIS FILMS.
+ 52 (81) 1255.0397
HELLO @ NEMESISNEMESIS.COM
NEMESISNEMESIS.COM

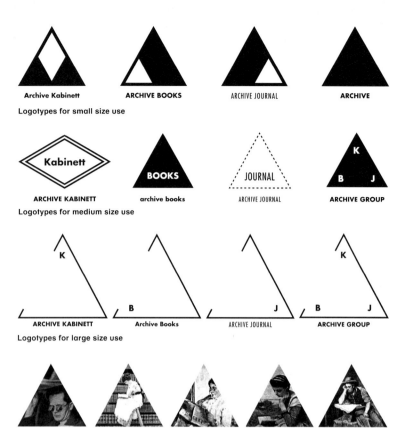

Logotypes for small size use

Archive Kabinett · ARCHIVE BOOKS · ARCHIVE JOURNAL · ARCHIVE

Logotypes for medium size use

ARCHIVE KABINETT · archive books · ARCHIVE JOURNAL · ARCHIVE GROUP

Logotypes for large size use

ARCHIVE KABINETT · Archive Books · ARCHIVE JOURNAL · ARCHIVE GROUP

Accompanying logotypes

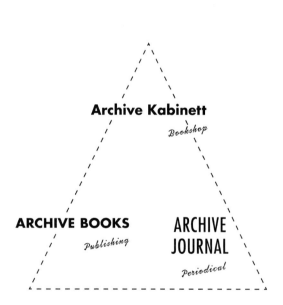

Archive Kabinett
Bookshop

ARCHIVE BOOKS
Publishing

ARCHIVE JOURNAL
Periodical

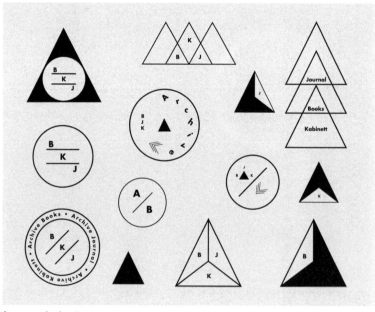

Accompanying logotypes

PAGES 242–245

Archive Books

Berlin, Germany

Delphine Dubuisson, 2011

Archive is more than a publishing house, book store, and gallery space. It is a platform for artistic and cultural research, debate, and self-education, dedicated to contemporary cultural production. Its members are designers, editors, artists, translators, and interns who work collectively, splitting up tasks according to competences, and workspaces according to projects. Its activities add up to a movement or flow: Archive Appendix is a design office and the birthplace of the organisation's iconic black-and-white branding, which represents Archive's different facets and projects by means of a variety of icons and word marks. Archive Kabinett is a meeting place devoted to exchange and research and at the same time the headquarters of Archive Books and Archive Journal, which publish and distribute the various findings and results of Archive's work.

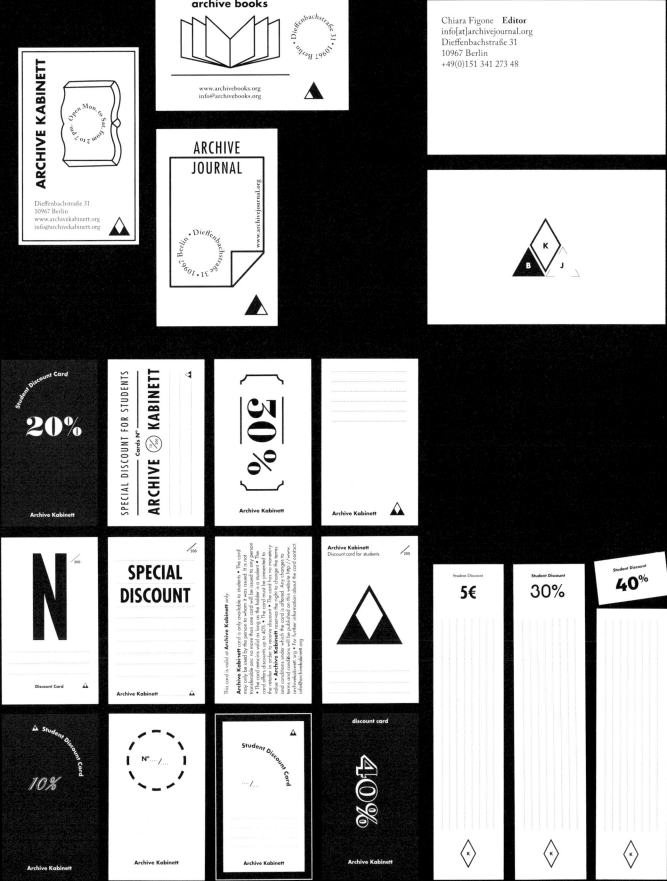

archive books

www.archivebooks.org
info@archivebooks.org

ARCHIVE KABINETT

Open Mon. to Sat. from 2 to 7 pm.

Dieffenbachstraße 31
10967 Berlin
www.archivekabinett.org
info@archivekabinett.org

ARCHIVE JOURNAL

Dieffenbachstraße 31 · 10967 Berlin · www.archivejournal.org

Chiara Figone   **Editor**
info[at]archivejournal.org
Dieffenbachstraße 31
10967 Berlin
+49(0)151 341 273 48

Student Discount Card
20%
Archive Kabinett

SPECIAL DISCOUNT FOR STUDENTS
ARCHIVE KABINETT
Cards N° 13/200

50%
Archive Kabinett

Archive Kabinett

N /200
Discount Card

SPECIAL DISCOUNT
Archive Kabinett

This card is valid at **Archive Kabinett** only.

Archive Kabinett card is only available to students • The card may only be used by the person to whom it was issued. It is not transferable and no more than one card will be issued to any person • The card remains valid as long as the holder is a student • The card offers discounts up to 40% • The card must be presented to the retailer in order to receive discount • The card has no monetary value • **Archive Kabinett** reserves the right to change the terms and conditions under which the card is offered. Any changes to terms and conditions will be published on this website http://www.archivekabinett.org • For further information about the card contact: info@archivekabinett.org

Archive Kabinett
Discount card for students   /200

△ Student Discount Card
10%
Archive Kabinett

N°..../....
Archive Kabinett

Student Discount Card
..../....
Archive Kabinett

discount card
40%
Archive Kabinett

Student Discount
5€

Student Discount
30%

Student Discount
40%

14-16 October 2010

Archive Kabinett ▲

Temporary bookshop

ARCHIVE KABINETT's purpose is to create a space to experiment with formats and concepts related to the publishing field, to stimulate a challenging collaboration between artists, writers and curators while exploring their roles. Archive Kabinett aims not only at fostering art but also at defining and developing a platform for art publishing. Its intent is to present the viewer with thought-provoking events, to encourage a critical discussion around "contemporary culture" through artists lectures, exhibitions and talks and to promote curiosity for every field. Devoted to research and reflection on artistic, social, and political practices, Archive Kabinett aims to translate, organize, and circulate theoretical materials. Archive Kabinett is the headquarters of Archive Books and Archive Journal.

www.archivekabinett.org – info@archivekabinett.org – Dieffenbachstraße 31. 10967 Berlin

ARCHIVE KABINETT

•

Temporary bookshop

AT **SUNDAY** FAIR **LONDON**
FROM **14** TO **16 OCTOBER 2010**

ARCHIVE KABINETT's purpose is to create a space to experiment with formats and concepts related to the publishing field, to stimulate a challenging collaboration between artists, writers and curators while exploring their roles. Archive Kabinett aims not only at fostering art but also at defining and developing a platform for art publishing. Its intent is to present the viewer with thought-provoking events, to encourage a critical discussion around "contemporary culture" through artists lectures, exhibitions and talks and to promote curiosity for every field. Devoted to research and reflection on artistic, social, and political practices, Archive Kabinett aims to translate, organize, and circulate theoretical materials. Archive Kabinett is the headquarters of Archive Books and Archive Journal.

www.archivekabinett.org – info@archivekabinett.org – Dieffenbachstraße 31. 10967 Berlin

18.09 — 18. 12.11

. Berlin  →

istanbul

↓

budapest

INVENTORY,

CZECH REP.

A **PROJECT** BY

GREECE

ARCHIVE KABINETT FOR THE
THESSALONIKI BIENNÁLE

↓

HUNGARY

↓

TURKEY

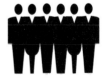

praha

↓

. Thessaloniki

POLAND

warszawa

http://www.archivekabinett.org

Ghetto Film School
New York City, USA

Attack, 2010

The Ghetto Film School, or GFS, is a non-profit institution in the South Bronx that provides high school students with the unique resources and opportunities for creating their own narrative films. Attack designed a new, comprehensive identity and fully integrated branding system based on Gaffa tape, an elementary tool of the film industry.

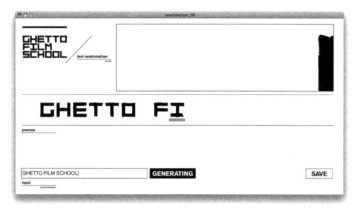

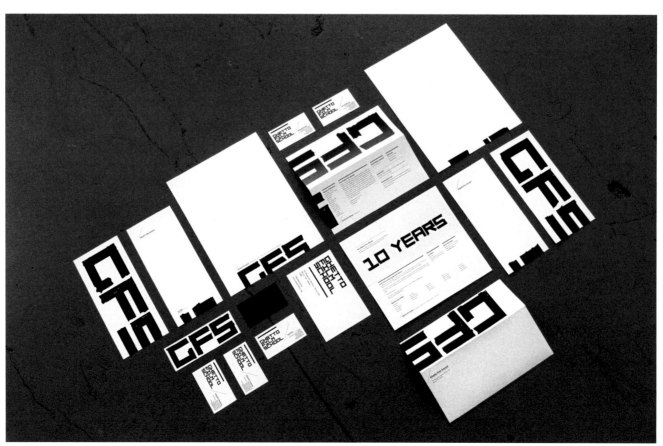

THIRDROW FILMS

THIRDROW FILMS

Thirdrow Films

Melbourne, Australia

21-19, 2009

Operating under the name of Thirdrow Films, Nigel Karikari and Olivia Peniston-Bird write, direct, produce, and post produce feature films, commercials, music videos, and corporate communication.

Offering exceptional production values, original thinking, and the commitment to exceed expectations, they sought an outstanding and highly individual identity solution to represent their small handpicked team. Commissioned with the task, 21-19 focused on how Nigel Karikari and Olivia Peniston-Bird first met: in the third row of a cinema. Inspired by the personal story of the company's founders, a row of chairs became the key image of the identity. Used within the context of seemingly random landscape photographs it expresses Thirdrow Film's versatility and the artistic value of unexpected, unconventional ideas.

Kaki
Restaurant
Brussels, Belgium

Pam&Jenny, 2009

Kaki is a rather unconventional restaurant in Brussels that serves "mobile food for creative people," in the form of a large and variable range of small portions of healthy food.

Taking the limitations of a very low budget project as an opportunity rather than a restriction, Pam&Jenny created a very distinct interior, consisting of an artful composition of fondly selected vintage chairs and lamps, painted garden tables, and illustrated apartment mock-ups on the walls. A number of flea market dog figures and figurines are scattered around the restaurant as protagonists of Kaki's graphic identity.

The Flower Appreciation Society

London, UK

Anna Day and Ellie Jauncey, 2011

When Day and Jauncey first met they immediately discovered their shared love of flowers. The seed for the Flower Appreciation Society was sown. Influenced by their creative background in illustration and textile design, they offer natural and sometimes quirky arrangements of local seasonal flowers, crafted in and delivered from their London workshop.

Unable to pay for a professional designer and a commercial font, Day and Jauncey developed their brand image by themselves. The handcrafted, very personal and distinctive result is not only a comme il faut example of DIY design, but also a visual expression of the Flower Appreciation Society's tagline "not your average florists." Every word, every letter is unique, just like every bouquet and every flower.

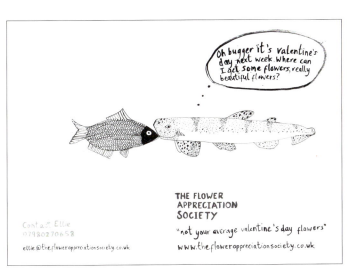

Designer Index

Introducing:

Visual Identities for Small Businesses

Edited by Robert Klanten, Sven Ehmann, and Anna Sinofzik
Text by Anna Sinofzik

Cover and layout by Floyd E. Schulze for Gestalten
Cover images by Anagrama, Arts and Recreation, Bond, Bunch, Dan Blackman, Codefrisko, Concrete, Deutsche & Japaner, Pam&Jenny, Pure Magenta, and Tayburn
Typeface: Helvetica Textbook by Linotype Design Studio

Project management by Julian Sorge for Gestalten
Production management by Janine Milstrey for Gestalten
Proofreading by Bettina Klein
Printed by Graphicom Slr
Made in Europe
Published by Gestalten, Berlin 2012
ISBN 978-3-89955-411-3

For more information, please visit www.gestalten.com.

Bibliographic information published by the Deutsche Nationalbibliothek.
    The Deutsche Nationalbibliothek lists this publication in the Deutsche Nationalbibliografie; detailed bibliographic data are available online at http://dnb.d-nb.de.

None of the content in this book was published in exchange for payment by commercial parties or designers; Gestalten selected all included work based solely on its artistic merit.

This book was printed on paper certified by the FSC®.

MIX
Paper from responsible sources
FSC® C013123

Gestalten is a climate-neutral company. We collaborate with the non-profit carbon offset provider myclimate (www.myclimate.org) to neutralize the company's carbon footprint produced through our worldwide business activities by investing in projects that reduce CO_2 emissions (www.gestalten.com/myclimate).